FLYING JOYFULLY

The Polly Usher Story

BY

Polly Usher

Book Publishers Network
Bothell • WA • 98041
and
Romar Enterprises
P. O. Box 2254
Palm Springs • CA • 92263
(760) 327-8125

10 9 8 7 6 5 4 3 2
First Edition
Printed in the United States of America

LCCN 2005927105
ISBN 1-887542-26-4

Cover Design: Laura Zugzda
Interior Layout: Stephanie Martindale
Proofreader: Julie Scandora

It is with love and affection that I dedicate this book to my daughter Wendy, my two lovely granddaughters Erika and Michelle, all of my wonderful relatives and friends who have been a part of my life, making it a happy, interesting journey and to all of my students who flew so safely.

CONTENTS

ACKNOWLEDGEMENTS

I am grateful to my daughter, Wendy and granddaughters, Erika and Michelle who assisted with my many notes. Deep appreciation and thanks go to Marie Robertson whose dedication was crucial in bringing my story to publication. We share a love of flying in the wild blue yonder in small aircrafts. She took my notes, promoted the upcoming publication of my book, and kept me "Flying Joyfully" in my retirement. Special thanks to Catherine Nelson who introduced me to Marie, Rosemary Smith, Linda LaCombe and Sheryn Hara. And I will never forget the many people who attended my lectures and requested my First Edition in advance. Thank you ALL.

I want to express my gratitude to Suzy Meyer, Publisher, Cortez Journal/Cortez Sentinel/Montezuma Valley Publishing for granting me permission to use any stories or pictures as indicated in my book. And to The Old Bold Pilots, The Palm Springs Air Museum, Southwest Airlines, *The Desert Sun*, Smithsonian Institution, The National Air and Space Society Wall of Honor, National Air and Space Museum, Washington, D.C. for their recognition of my contribution to aviation.

I have enjoyed my flying adventures and returning in memory to the wonderful places I encountered and friends who are still a part of my life. If I have failed to mention anyone or place, I apologize, and hope you will forgive me.

PROLOGUE

There are countless stories "out there" remaining untold because either the thought never occurred to anyone to set them into print or, as in many cases, it just did not catch the eye of a prospective publisher. The Polly Usher story is one of these.

Today, January 2005, Polly Usher, tall and lean is 89, and meeting her was a pleasure that I shall always remember. She is lively, alert, has a sparkling smile from ear to ear when she relates her experience, delighting her listeners.

Her accomplishments commencing in 1937 to the present are amazing. It is a surprise that her story had not found its way into print for others to read. Her scrapbook alone reveals the extent of her experiences. When my friend, Catherine Nelson, and nearby neighbor of Polly Usher, asked me if I had time to meet Polly, I was not sure what to expect.

Polly, with the aid of her daughter, Wendy, had spent many hours typing up some material. I am grateful to them for allowing me the privilege of taking on the responsibility of getting "The Polly Usher Story" in book form. An attempt has been made to retain the simplicity of Polly's own style as she prepared her notes. There is no particular chronological order to her many adventures as they are related in the book. Rather, it is Polly as she remembers and tells her story, but it is historically illuminating about a time long past. I believe the book will be highly received by those who know her, by those interested in the early days of flying an airplane, those interested in the early days of World War II where she trained some of the first pilots, and the early filming days where she flew over Monument Valley, Utah assisting film crews with location sites. Her recognition by the Smithsonian Institution in Washington, D. C. and her mention in a Southwest Airlines Magazine, and her significant meetings with some notables as she flew around the country, attest to her accomplishments. Polly's achievements are awesome when one considers her story begins back in 1937. In those days, the idea of flying was not expected to last, let alone that a woman—Polly Usher—got her Pilot's License, Instructor's License, Commercial License and went on to contribute so much at a crucial time in the United States and abroad during the early days of World War II.

Doing this project is more an admiration and respect for a fine lady who I feel should have "Her Book". I am well aware of the excitement of flying as I, too, spent my share of hours being in the "wild blue yonder". I know when anyone meets Polly, listens to her lectures and sees those sparkling eyes darting with excitement as she talks, you would feel the same. So, this simple but fascinating bit of flying history is not only for the reader, but especially for YOU, Polly. Here's to you and that ever-captivating wild blue yonder we both so enjoyed.

Marie Robertson
Palm Springs, California

POLLY USHERED AVIATION INTO CORTEZ

That was the headline in the Cortez, Colorado, local newspaper. I am that pilot: Polly Usher. In this year 2005, I am eighty-nine years old—yes, an old timer with a personal story along with some historical facts. Hopefully, it will afford additional insight into the past —especially when it comes to the early days of flying—and the incredible feat that we have accomplished conquering the air by sending aloft magnificent flying machines. To top it off, women became a part of that flying—long before women's liberation and recognition existed. My story is written in an easy-to-read simple style, but I hope you will enjoy the antics of a really early woman flyer. It was 1937 when I met and married Rollin Usher, and that was only the beginning of how my life would change. Our love for each other was only slightly overshadowed by the great love of flying that we developed through the years. As any pilot and most if not all would readily admit to, this was love—love of truly being "in the clouds" with "wings" no less!

Yes, this is my story, but to the modern generation of 2005, it will take you back to a whole different time not only in some of the flying tales of the very, very early years, but to some of the happenings in the United States at a crucial time before and during the breakout of World War II. And this story is not just about me but also about the many young people of that day who went through an unforgettable era.

Rollins'
First →
Airplane
Ride - 1916
His Remark:
Yes, That is
Me holding
on with My
Finger Tips -

AND SO IT BEGINS

We were married on August 9, 1937, and I was happily beginning a new life. There I was, wife of the local bank president, Rollin Usher, in the small town of Cortez—the Four Corners area—so named because it is a unique area in the United States. Four states come together at one point namely: Colorado, New Mexico, Utah and Arizona. There was always some sort of unexplained pride in that fact!

Early one morning a few months after our marriage Rollin and I were walking around our home area observing the beautiful Colorado sky and white fluffy cumulus clouds overhead. This was a morning ritual—it gave us a special closeness to start the day. We

3

had exchanged a few lingering kisses and hugs, seemingly asking for more. But after one more brief moment, he would go off to his position at the bank. I would head inside and start the daily household chores.

But in this particular moment, something was different. What we were amazed to see as we looked upward into the great blue yonder, was a small, yellow plane flying overhead. This was a very rare sight in 1937 and in our area! It circled the town, then headed for a small strip of land east of the town. Without hesitation we jumped into our car and went to where the plane landed.

There sat this 40-horsepower, two-seater Piper Cub airplane. Alongside it stood a happy, red-haired pilot smiling from ear to ear! We were overwhelmed and excited like two little kids. He didn't have to ask us twice if we wanted to go for a ride. Rollin as a young boy had saved enough money to get a ride on a small plane, so he was raring to get up there again. No question, we were both ready to go up into that sky.

As it was only a two-seater where the pilot and passenger sat one in front of the other, Rollin said, "well, ok, ladies first, honey." So up and inside I went.

I was strapped in. The pilot applied power to the engine and, after gaining some speed, gently lifted the plane over the three-foot fence at the end of the grass strip, and we were IN the air. FLYING. I could not believe it!

We circled over Cortez, and I found myself looking down at the countryside, our home, and the main street. It did not take long to persuade me that washing dishes and dusting furniture was suddenly very unimportant. My soul became part of this magnificent exposure and a great awareness of how much more there really is to life. I was ecstatic, and knew at once my life would not be the same.

Rollin completed his ride, and as he got out of the plane and approached me, we knew instinctively BOTH our lives would be changed. We were, indeed, like two kids in a special cloud of their own, dreaming about flying. "Maybe," Rollin said, "we can talk the pilot into staying and giving us flying lessons." Without hesitation I replied, "Let's do it, let's do it." And so at that moment a new life began for both of us. But never in my wildest imagination would I have thought that one day this would lead to viewing my name on The Wall of Honor at the Smithsonian Air and Space Museum in Washington, D. C.—as an early-time female pilot who had contributed to the growth of aviation in the U.S.A.

The instructor explained to us that if we wanted to learn to fly, we would have to take our lessons very early in the morning. Cortez is located at an altitude of 6200 feet, and the airstrip was only a hundred feet in length. There is some lift for the airplane in cool air, but as soon as the air becomes warm, this advantage is lost.

Truly, I was a dedicated student—I was totally mesmerized with excitement. I awoke each morning at the crack of dawn and quietly crept out of bed so as not to disturb my husband. I dressed quickly and headed for the airstrip. There he was, our instructor, Carl Darnall, waiting beside a small bonfire he had built to keep himself warm until I arrived.

I quickly climbed into the plane while he spun the propellor to start the engine. I advanced the throttle gently to keep the engine running as he had instructed me to do until he was able to climb into the cockpit. Then he advanced full throttle and started the take-off, lifting the plane deftly over the fence at the end of the airstrip by easing back on the stick to get the plane airborne. I observed every action. I was fascinated, and I KNEW that some-day I would be accomplishing the procedure by myself.

On my first lesson I discovered that flying just straight and level was not as easy as I had thought it would be. The slightest movement in the air currents changed the altitude of the airplane. My feet, which were placed on the rudder pedals, controlled the movement of the rear of the plane and had to be coordinated with a movement of the stick in the same direction, which maneuvered the wings and front of the aircraft. But, it did not take long before I got the feel of it—a touch which has never left me. My first words at this delightful experience were "hey, groovey," which today would probably translate into "cool."

Instructor Carl Darnall was a very early-time pilot (bearing in mind I'm writing about 1937), with the Airman's license number of 63.

The airplane he flew at that time was very unreliable, and the engine often would quit while he was flying. He already had had the experience of forty or more forced-landings—landing his plane in a field, on a road, or wherever he could locate an accessible spot allowing him to land without engine power. He wanted me to have the knowledge to cope with any and all emergencies that might happen while piloting a plane. Consequently, every so often when I was circling the airstrip in preparation for a landing, he would turn the engine off, forcing me to make what was called a "dead-stick" landing. Believe me, there were many anxious and exciting moments. Here I was, a young woman in 1937, learning to fly when it was rare for women to work outside the home let alone pilot a plane

If the early morning air was cool enough so that we could gain sufficient altitude, I had lessons on doing "spins." This was done by easing back on the throttle, pulling the nose of the aircraft into a stall, and applying full pressure on the right rudder for a right-hand spin, or pressure on the left rudder for a left-hand spin. At that point the airplane would spin toward the ground at a rapid speed. To recover, the pilot had to apply engine power and ease back on the stick, bringing the plane back to level flight. Rather than being frightened, I found myself exhilarated. It WAS exciting to feel myself headed toward the earth and yet be in control of bringing the plane back from a dangerous situation to level and flying happily again. I loved it.

This particular morning was beautiful; not a breeze was blowing through the trees. I thought, "Great day." Carl greeted me but quickly announced that he was extremely busy and my lesson would be a short one. As disappointed as I was, I tried not to show it. He followed me out to the airplane and then simply said, "Ok. Polly, you take her up off the ground. I'm going to be your passenger. Follow the traffic pattern as I taught you and make a landing." I was taken aback at first, thinking how I enjoyed our full thirty minutes of flight instruction. But I did as Carl instructed, took the little aircraft into the air, and reached an altitude of four hundred feet, flying parallel to the field. Since it would be my only opportunity for a landing that day, I planned to really impress my passenger/instructor and make it a good one. After we landed, Carl got out of the plane and said, "Well, Polly, it's all yours; take the plane up by yourself and make another great landing like the last one." I couldn't believe it! I was going to be alone, flying by myself! I was just bursting with excitement.

There I was, filled with all sorts of happy butterflies as I taxied down the end of the airstrip. I turned the plane for a takeoff, applied power to the engine, and when I felt it was right, eased back on the stick and left the ground. The rush of joy and elation is difficult to describe. It consumed my whole personality as I smiled and smiled and smiled. I WAS flying—flying by myself. Those birds had nothing on me. Oh how I had admired their flight when I was a child. Bird-watching was fun for me, but now I was flying through the air. I did not want those moments in the air to end. I wanted them to go on forever. And I thought of Rollin...wait until he hears this!

Mrs. R. N. Usher, Student Flyer, Made Solo Flight Tuesday A. M.

Mrs. Usher First Lady To Fly Solo at Cortez

To Mrs. R. N. Usher goes the credit for being the first Cortez lady to fly a plane solo, having made her initial flight Tuesday after a little over eleven hours in the air, under instructions of Instructor Carl Darnall. Mrs. Usher has been practicing landing for the past week and Tuesday took the ship up by herself, taking off, flying and landing in perfect form. She repeated the act Wednesday.

While it is well established Mrs. Usher is the first woman to fly solo at Cortez, it is entirely possible she is the first of the women in the entire Basin to do so, and she is being complimented by many friends.

Another flying enthusiast who "took wing on his own" this week was Reuben Springmeyer who soloed Wednesday. He too made it up and down, and back to his work at Mexirado Distributing Company. Reuben had had just the minimum time required for student, 8 hours and 15 minutes.

To Mrs. Polly Usher, wife of R. N. Usher, cashier of the Citizens State Bank, goes the distinction of being the first woman flying student in western Colorado to make a solo flight, as nearly as a check-up on available records will disclose.

Mrs. Usher earned her "wings" when she took the Cub training ship of the Cortez Air School off the local airport Tuesday morning and after circling about the field for several minutes brought it down to a graceful landing that would have been a credit to an experienced pilot.

She had eleven hours and twenty minutes instruction before making her solo, Instructor C. V. 'Red' Darnall said. She has been the most diligent student he has ever had, he states, putting in time at the controls that men who are beginning to fly will seldom tackle.

By making her solo flight Tuesday, Mrs. Usher beat her husband, who is also taking lessons, by two days. Mr. Usher made his solo flight this morning. He has had approximately five hours instruction from Darnall touching up on his previous air training.

Reuben Springmeyer, Mexirado Dist. Co. truck driver, made his solo Wednesday and established a record for the school in the least number of hours instruction before his solo flight.

[...] quite [...] in students making their first solo. As one flyer stated recently, any [...] license al- [...] at once.

If Mrs. Usher continues flying as she intends to do, until she receives her license, she will be one of a very few licensed women pilots in the state of Colorado. At present there are only three, all of whom are living in Denver. It appears likely therefore, that Mrs. Usher will be the first on the western slope.

FIRST WOMAN FLYING STUDENT
IN WESTERN COLORADO

This report was published in the local newspaper the next day:

> To Mrs. Polly Usher, wife of R. N. Usher, Cashier of Citizens State Bank, goes the distinction of being the first woman flying student in Western Colorado to make a solo flight.
>
> Mrs. Usher earned her "wings" when she took the Cub Training Ship of Cortez Air School off the Local Air Strip, Tuesday morning, and after circling about the field for several minutes, brought the aircraft down to a graceful landing that would have been a credit to an

experienced pilot. C. C. Darnall, instructor, said, 'Polly has been the most diligent student I've ever had, putting time at the controls that most men who are beginning to fly will seldom tackle."

Flying from the local airport was really quite an undertaking. It required a lot more skill than just the usual flying skills, especially in students making their first solo. As one flyer said, "Any student who can make a solo from this field deserves a license almost at once."

WE ARE A FLYING COUPLE

My solo flight was behind me. I was a pilot! I will always remember the enthusiastic congratulations from my instructor and, quite frankly, how hard it was for me to literally bring my body back to earth. Telling Rollin of my accomplishment was all I could think of next. I can still see him looking at me—no words were necessary—my face, eyes, and body said it all. Rollin just looked at me opened his arms and said, "You did it; you soloed. I am so happy for you, Polly."

Two days later he had the same wonderful experience when he made his first solo flight. We felt renewed and celebrated a new way of living. We both knew that many adventures lay ahead of us, but there were some bumps ahead as well!

On Rollin's second solo flight, his mind was wandering on how much he liked to fly that he literally "forgot" to fly and forgot to apply power to the engine when the aircraft touched the ground as we had been instructed to do. Consequently, the front of the plane tipped over, hitting the ground and breaking the propellor. As a result the only plane in the area was out of commission until a new propellor could be obtained and installed. The flying enthusiasts had fun chiding Rollin as "crash Usher."

Rollin was always a progressive thinker. His thoughts went to the idea that perhaps we could start a business venture connected to flying. Cortez was in an isolated area with very minimal bus transportation, and the nearest railroad was one hundred miles away in Gallup, New Mexico. If we could purchase a plane large enough to accommodate passengers, our instructor could fly them to Denver and surrounding area airports. It would be the beginning of a small airline service.

We located a Ryan Aircraft that was for sale. It was a sister-ship to the "Spirit of St. Louis"—the plane which Charles Lindbergh flew solo across the Atlantic Ocean in 1927. The cost of the plane was six hundred dollars. I, being a very conservative person was unwilling to go into debt for that amount of money, but my husband was a very persuasive man. I loved Rollin dearly, so naturally I ended up agreeing to the start of this new project and expense.

The bank loaned us the six hundred dollars, and the Ryan aircraft was ours. The plane was brought to our small airstrip and we were like two kids in an ice cream shop. We were beyond excited as we faced this venture. The people in Cortez were just as interested and enthusiastic. Having an air service that would eliminate long drives on the curving highway through the fourteen-thousand-foot-high mountains between the western slope of Colorado and Denver would be a big advantage to the community.

But it was not all that easy. Our venture became short-lived as our excitement got the best of us. There was a large group of flying enthusiasts around, admiring our plane. Rollin got into the cockpit to practice taxiing the airplane on the ground. I was in the seat behind him to witness the procedure. He applied power to the engine very carefully, but he was not accustomed to the hand brakes on the plane and accidentally pulled the wrong one. Whereas he expected to make a turn to the left which was the direction of the airstrip, the plane turned instead abruptly to the right into our car, which was parked nearby, causing considerable damage to plane and car. Rollin turned around to face me—pale and shocked. He was dejected and said, "Polly, I don't have enough sense to pour it out of a boot." I agreed with him, but only momentarily, as I knew him to be a man who could tackle any challenge in spite of any adversity. Our friends who had watched the entire episode called out, "Crash Usher strikes again," and there was laughter instead of disaster—after all no one was injured.

So there we were without a plane, without a car, and we still owed the bank six hundred dollars. Undaunted, we resumed our flying in the four-horse powered Cub plane and obtained our thirty-five hours of solo flight time—a requirement for a full private pilot's license at that time. We both passed the written test and the final flight test. And did we ever celebrate when we received that official license! This allowed us to take up passengers in the plane along with us but not for hire—that would require two hundred solo hours and another flight and written test to obtain the commercial license. Since we did not have our own aircraft at that time, where could we put all this passion we had to fly—where could we go from here with no plane of our own?

We lived in a lovely home built for us by my father as our wedding present. Father was a building contractor. One evening Rollin sat alongside me with pad and pencil in hand. "Do you realize," he stated, "that it is costing us sixty-dollars a month with taxes and upkeep to live in our own home? One of my customers at the bank has built a new house that he will rent to us for only thirty dollars a month. So if we sold our home, we would have enough money to buy a small airplane and start traveling by air." We looked at each other—the flying twinkle was in our eyes. It was a big extra hunk of love between us—this flying bug! "Sounds good to me," I heard myself saying, "but we should talk to Father about it first. Except for his generosity and love, we would not have this house." Rollin agreed that we should take our idea to Father. And Father was great about it. He had also read the newspaper articles and knew how much we loved flying and how hard we had worked to get our license. All he said was, "If that is what you want to do, do it. Just be sure that wherever you live, you have a bedroom for your mother and me when we come to visit." Well, now, how lucky can two people get? Rollin and I had never ever forgotten that one, big, first start with Father's help.

We rented the house. It had a bedroom on the first floor and one down in the basement near the furnace. Rollin and I chose to sleep in the basement bedroom, leaving the main bedroom available for my parents who were then able to arrive at any time. They had given us an opportunity no one else would have ever been able to do for us.

FAMILY BACKGROUND

My mother and father were both born in Denmark in the 1800's. They first met in their early teens when they were both part of a group of youths playing in the streets of the city of Allborg in the early evenings. My father was instantly intrigued with this lovely young girl who was later to be my mother.

One evening as curfew sounded, he ran up to her and kissed her on the cheek. Since this was a very bold thing to do at that time, he then ran as fast as he could toward home. Within his home was a permanently angry, grumpy father who resented any happiness displayed by his son and took out his frustration by sitting in a chair with a large, sturdy stick beside him, ready to throw it at the boy as soon as he returned and opened the door. However, this young boy had a very quick mind, and his body responded to his thinking, so as soon as he stepped inside, he rapidly evaded the thrown missile, ran into the kitchen to grab some food, and then bolted to his bedroom where he could be alone with his thoughts and dreams. This became a ritual which he accepted as part of his life.

There was little love shown in his family, but the next evening he was back on the street playing with his friends, and directing all of his love to my mother-to-be. He realized at their first meeting that she was the love of his life, and a few years later they were engaged to be married.

My father, Alfred Christian Larsen had completed only the fourth grade when his father removed him from school and apprenticed him out to a local bricklayer to learn that trade. As soon as he had completed this training and was now able to support himself, his dream was to go to America—which everyone knew was the "Land of Freedom and Opportunity." Although he only spoke and understood the Danish language, he did not consider that a hindrance. His confidence assured him that once he was living in America, he would be able to promptly learn the English language by listening to the words as they were spoken and absorbing the meaning of them in his mind.

As soon as he could save enough money from his meager wage to purchase a ticket on a boat, he took off, promising my mother, Else Marie, whom he called Mary because it was easy to pronounce and because she was such a "merry," fun-loving person, that he would send for her soon. He landed at Ellis Island in New York, and when he had completed the Immigration Process, went to Worcester, Massachusetts where one of my mother's aunt had a dairy business and lovely home. He worked at odd jobs until he had earned enough money to send for his beloved fiancée. They were married in a small Danish Lutheran Church, and ten months later my oldest sister, Alma Margaret, was born.

At this time, my father became intrigued with the slogan: "Go west young man, go west." Although he did not have enough money for a train ticket, this was another dream which he intended to follow. Leaving my mother with her relatives, he went to the nearest train station, hopped on a westbound train, and joined the hobos or bums, as they were named. These were men who wanted to start living in a different part of the country and, also, had no money to purchase a ticket for transportation. While the train was stopped at a railroad station, they would sneak quietly into the baggage section, hoping desperately that they would not be discovered by railroad employees and thrown off the train. They huddled together while the train was traveling, and whenever the train pulled into a station for a short stop, they would look out of the compartment, and when they thought they would not be observed, went to nearby homes to ask for food. My father always insisted on doing some small chore in payment for food which was given to him. In later years, whenever anyone came to our home asking for food, he would treat them with great respect, giving them a meal and food to take with them for their next meal. They were always so grateful as never had they received such kind treatment. But because my father had experienced hunger and had been without money himself, he always was willing to share.

During the train trip across the country, the men traveling in the baggage compartment developed a camaraderie and loyalty, which later was to become a salvation for my father. When he reached Denver, saw the beautiful Colorado mountains and the gorgeous scenery, and breathed the wonderful fresh air, he knew immediately that this Mile High City was where he wanted to live and raise a family. He went to the nearest Western Union office and wired my mother, "This is it. Come to Denver on the next train." He was so caught up in the excitement of having found the perfect destination that he quickly ran back out into the street, leaving his billfold with all the money he possessed on the Western Union counter. When he returned a few minutes later, someone had already taken it. So there he was: my mother and their eighteen-month-old baby would be arriving soon, and he would not be able to rent a room where they could sleep. Immediately, one of his traveling companions came to his rescue by selling his overcoat and giving all of the money to my father. This was a wonderful favor for which he was forever grateful.

He was soon able to get a job as a bricklayer, and gather enough material to build a three-room house where they could start raising a family. When Alma was three years old, my sister Oda was born. Two years later, my sister Evelyn joined the family, and two years later, September 14, 1915, I arrived into this wonderful world. My birth was soon followed by the arrival of a little boy with dark, curly hair and beautiful, bright blue eyes, named Irving Ralph. I adored him at first sight, and we became inseparable, but his life was to be short. One day when I was four years old and he was not quite three, we wandered into a neighbor's yard and started eating fruit from their cherry tree. They were luscious and sweet. We ran around the tree, looking for cherries that we could reach, popping them quickly into our mouths. They were so delicious, and we kept eating until little Irving became suddenly ill. I grabbed his little hand and hurried back home with him. Mother called our doctor immediately, as they made house calls at that time. He arrived a short time later, but was unable to save the life of my darling brother, and he died that night. I was completely crushed and often still think of him. But God is good and always has seemed to know my needs, even as a small child, and my brother Thomas Alfred was born a year later. There was always a close bond between us. Then three years later another brother joined the family who was named Irving.

Whenever my mother became pregnant, my father would start adding another room to our house, so the neighbors were well aware when a baby was expected and were ready to help with the delivering when the baby arrived, as we were all born at home.

My father soon became a prominent building contractor in the Denver area and would deposit left-over supplies in our yard, which were used to build larger houses for our family.

As a child growing up I was mesmerized by the blue of the skies and the birds in flight. I often wonder now….was that the beginning of my inner desire to be up there in the clouds in the wild blue yonder? My mother would call for me and say, "Polly, when are you going to come in and do some chores?" I wondered, how could I do that when I was so immersed in the beauty of the Colorado sky?

School days in Denver were happy and carefree. I realized more and more as the years passed by just how fortunate I was to have attended a Manual Training High School. We had dedicated teachers who not only taught us the desire for learning but the skills needed to enhance our future lives. Very special friendships developed in those years. My closest friend, Mildred Longman, and I are inseparable even to this day.

In 1933 when I graduated, our country was in the midst of the great Depression. There was no money for college let alone any real needs. It was a struggle for Father to provide for us, but he was always ready to accept challenges. Subsequently, he decided to try farming in order to raise food for us. He purchased some land outside Denver and built a home that would accommodate all of us, including my oldest sister and her family, as they had no place to go due to conditions at that time during the Depression.

The depression years were an interesting experience as we all managed to survive through ingenuity and determination with no help from anyone. It was a far cry from today—2005—where all sorts of help is available during periods of crisis.

When President Franklin Roosevelt created the WPA program, it gave small towns the financing needed for new buildings, and eventually my father was able to get back into the construction business.

We moved to the little town of Cortez in 1936, and Father started construction on the County Court House. Soon the local banker, who was interested in the activities in the area, came to view the construction sites. So there he was, introducing himself to me inside our small construction office—my future husband! He was so handsome and seemingly so intelligent. We had some brief words, but they seemed to linger on our lips. He was hesitant to leave, and when I heard him ask me to join him for dinner, I was overwhelmed. I was very happy at this prospect.

Because the one restaurant in Cortez opened only for breakfast and lunch, we found ourselves driving forty miles on a winding road through the mountains to a popular eating place in Durango, Colorado. It was an exciting evening for me as we enjoyed the food, entertainment, and dancing. Before we knew it, it was 2 a.m. and well past my curfew. So by the time we drove up to the house, the porch light was on, alerting me that my parents were well aware of my late (early morning) arrival. I may have been twenty-one, but I was their daughter, and that was what was important. I remember

20

Rollin turning to me and saying, "What do you think they will say about your being so late?" I laughed and replied, "I am pretty certain they will insist that you marry me." But I was not concerned about my parents' reaction. As I walked in the house my father just said, "Did you have a good time?" So I went off to bed that night, knowing all would be well. This likeable handsome gentleman was accepted by my father. I could feel it.

We spent many days and evenings together. Compared to today's dating, it was simple, not as wild, but genuinely loving. One evening Rollin turned to me and said, "Do you think our ages will make any difference?"

I knew that Rollin was thirteen years older than I was, but I simply replied, "I really haven't noticed any difference."

To which he promptly replied, "Well then, will you marry me?"

"Yes," I answered without hesitation—he was special to me and I was special to him. You just could feel that sensation between the two of us. I wonder how many feel that today before they say the "I do"?

We made plans to visit Rollin's parents in Florence, Colorado, the first weekend following our engagement. I was rather apprehensive when we drove up in front of their home, but they both (Edith and Newell) were watching for us and came to our car with lovely smiles on their faces. We liked each other immediately.

Rollin had two sons from his previous marriage. Over the years I became friends with them, and their families are also an important part of my life today.

Florence, Colorado, was a lovely, small town with neatly painted houses, beautiful yards and gardens, and immense maple trees lining each street. The town residents were so proper—visiting each other at regular intervals, talking to each other so politely, and hosting an occasional backyard supper or game of bridge. Everyone was in bed by 10 p.m.

Rollins' parents loved to play bridge, but it was against their principles to play cards on a Sunday. Sometimes when we were visiting them only over the weekend, they would relent but would pull down all the shades, and we would play bridge practically in the dark. I was never quite sure if they were trying not to be seen by God or by their neighbors.

Rollin's boyhood friendships were close and lasting. Because there were no organized activities for children at that time, they made their own fun and had nicknames for everyone. Rollin was an only child and because his parents called him "Son," his nickname was "Sono." One boy was called "Hard Gravel" because at one time he had fallen on his face in the gravel and still had pits on his face caused by the hard pebbles. The town policeman was named "Rainbow" as he always showed up after the storm.

And, as most towns do, they also had their own "town character." His name was Taos McCandliss, a small, wiry, strong person with no visible means of support, and yet he could find ways of getting more than enough liquor to drink. When the weather began to get cold, he would get in a fight or cause enough disturbance to be put in jail for the winter where he had a place to stay and food to eat. When spring arrived he would be released to continue his happy existence. The stories concerning him were legend in the area. One of them was the following:

Part of the culture of this small town was the plays put on in the Opera House by traveling theater groups. Nearly everyone in town attended, dressed in their finest clothes. This particular night, "Uncle Tom's Cabin" was being presented. The Opera House was so silent a dropped pin could be heard as the audience watched, with tears in their eyes, the scene where the little white girl, who was dying, asked the black slave of the family, "Uncle Tom, Uncle Tom, what makes the grass so green?" In the complete silence, Taos McCandliss from the back row in the balcony, in his slightly drunken voice shouted, "Bullshit, Little Eva, bullshit," and Taos was taken to jail for the winter. I listened to many stories about Rollin's boyhood in this town and realized this background had contributed to his interesting personality.

After the happy, revealing weekend, I was convinced that our decision to marry was perfect. We returned to Cortez, and a short time later, because preparations for a wedding seemed too detailed for us, we drove to Santa Fe, New Mexico, obtained a marriage license, were married by a Methodist minister in his home, and spent a wonderful night in the bridal suite at the beautiful La Fonda Hotel. This was August 9, 1937.

So there it was: We met in June, became engaged in July, and married in August of the same year. The rest of the story is one of far more fulfillment than I could ever have imagined, and it all had to do with FLYING JOYFULLY, as we lived our life out together.

Grading Runways Aug. 30, 1942

MOVING UPWARD

Our home sold quickly and, without any regret, we moved our furniture and belongings into the rented house. We purchased some land two miles south of the town of Cortez so we would have an adequate airstrip and a place for a hangar in which to put the airplane we were planning to soon purchase.

I borrowed a tractor from a nearby farmer, and with the help of a few close lady friends, we had a hilarious time grading the land for a five-thousand-foot-length runway. Rollin had help from some of his construction buddies in building our hangar. Believe me, friendships in small towns, especially in those days, were amazing and a blessing. Everyone, it seemed, was eager for us to make progress in realizing our dreams. Eventually many became very enthusiastic about learning to fly. There were some private moments when I would think, "God, how lucky we are," because we were doing what we loved and having friends participate as well.

One of my friends, who had helped with making the landing airstrip, knew I was of Scandinavian background and, while we were resting one day, presented me with the following poem which she had written. It brought tears to my eyes and joy to my heart. It was written:

To a Pilot:

True child of that long-vanished Viking, like his, her spirit
Sings; but the seas she plies are the sun-swept skies, for her
Ship is a ship with wings.
Free air instead of wild water; instead of the waves, the wind;
Where the wild hawk wheels and the thunder peals till
The clouds have scattered and thinned.
Her eyes have the look of far spaces; they are confident, sure
Of her worth. Her proud head is high to the quickening sky,
For she's broken the fetters of the earth.

Taylorcraft BC12-D

This Taylorcraft comes in three models, varying with finish and equipment. All versions are equipped with a 65-h.p. Continental engine and have similar performance. Wing span is 36 feet. Maximum speed is 117 m.p.h., cruising speed 100 m.p.h., stalling speed 38 m.p.h. Cruising range varies with the model from 300 miles for the Standard to 505 miles for the DeLuxe. The Custom model (radio, fairing, lights, battery) sells for $2,600 f.a.f.; the DeLuxe (radio, battery, light fixtures) for $2,500 and the Standard Model (not hand-rubbed) for $2,400.

Photo courtesy of Taylorcraft Foundation

The Polly Usher Story

We were finally ready. Arrangements were made to purchase a two-place, sixty-five-horsepower Taylorcraft airplane from Combs-Hayden Aviation Company in Denver. Rollin had efficient employees at the bank so he could confidently take a month's vacation from his responsibilities there. We packed a few clothes and left Cortez on what was to be our last bus trip ever into Denver. We were on our way to pick up our new airplane! Then we were going to be enroute to the East Coast during which we would learn the happiness and responsibilities of traveling by air.

"Pansy" is the name we gave her, and she was a beauty! We fell in love at first sight as the colors of it were yellow and reddish brown which reminded us of some of the pansies that grew in our flower garden. The instruments in the plane consisted of a compass, altimeter (which measures the elevation of the plane above the ground), and an air speed indicator.

When our purchase transaction was completed, we climbed into our new plane and started taxiing to the end of the runway to begin our takeoff into the wind. We noticed the gas tank was only half-full and looked over to the gas-pump area where a customer was already waiting patiently to get his plane serviced. After a short consultation between us, we decided that we were eager to take off and did not want to be delayed; therefore, we would just land at an airstrip enroute as marked on our air map as being only fifty miles away east of Denver. We would fill up there.

Cautiously, we made our takeoff, being aware of the local air traffic. As soon as we were flying alone headed east toward our destination, we were so excited and overwhelmed. We exchanged big smiles and a few loving kisses. Talk about feeling like two kids who had taken more candy than they should have out of a jar…that was us! The joy I felt—we both felt—is something dear to my heart even to this day and age, January 2005. We were starting our journey together not only as husband and wife but as two licensed pilots with our own airplane—something almost unheard of in those days. This lift of happiness coincided very nicely with the same lift we felt as we left the airfield and gained altitude into the wild blue yonder.

Our exuberance was soon to diminish for, as we arrived at the airstrip where we had expected to fuel our plane, we looked below and noticed it had been converted to a farm with tall stalks of corn beneath us and no airstrip insight! Calmly, I examined the air map and detected another small airport a short distance away so we continued onward and, again, were surprised to find that it had been converted into a Pitch and Putt golf course. Neither of us panicked, but a slight aura of concern did appear on our faces. Finally, we located another airstrip and hastily landed to fill the gas tank. Within those two hours we learned two of our most valuable lessons:

Lesson #1—always have a full tank of gas on departure and

Lesson #2—be sure your air map is up-to-date.

Generally, I was in charge of navigation while my husband was doing the piloting of the plane. At that time there were no radios in the planes. We flew by the "Iron Compass" which was following the railroad tracks or dead-reckoning, using an air map which showed towns and elevations. I would use check points on the ground to determine the wind-drift.

The first air map firm was founded in Denver in the year 1933. Before that, aviation was a matter of:

- Knowing the railroad tracks, water towers, buildings, canyons, and other local landmarks.

- Getting verbal information from other pilots such as: "Don't pass that beacon to the left, or you will smack into a hill."
- Checking the roofs of buildings for the painted name of the town. It was a practice often done to aid pilots and very helpful to me, to determine where we were at all times.

August 1941

FASCINATED BY NEW ENGLAND

"Flying Couple" on Brief Vacation Here

New England is by far the most fascinating section of the United States from the air, in the eyes of Mr. and Mrs. Rollin Usher of Cortez, Col., who set down their Taylorcraft plane a few days ago at the North Grafton Airport, to spend a brief vacation with Mr. and Mrs. Lorance P. Salmonsen of 7 Victoria avenue, and Mr. and Mrs. Christian T. Salmonsen of 120 Forest street.

The profusion of lakes, rivulets and vegetation which offers a constant variety of scenic beauties to New England fliers, has spoiled the young aviator and his wife, whose native state is only sparsely endowed with scenic features, in their opinion. Their admiration, however, is daunted by the fact that Worcester as one of New England's representative cities and industrial centers does not own and operate an airport comparable to its status as a municipal center and important geographical position.

["Worcester has the] record [of being the] biggest city with the poorest airport in the country," Mr. Usher stated. "We have landed on fields in little towns with not more than a population of two thousand, which would shame your fair city. Yes, I believe without reservation, that Worcester has the poorest landing field in the country for a city its size," the flier asserted.

Mr. Usher and his wife speak with authority, since both have their private pilot's licenses and

"FLYING COUPLE"

Mr. and Mrs. Rollin Usher, the "flying couple" from Cortez, Col., who have been guests of Mr. and Mrs. Lorance P. Salmonsen of 7 Victoria avenue, and Mr. and Mrs. Christian T. Salmonsen of 120 Forest street.

FIRST SOLO CROSS-COUNTRY – EASTWARD

We finally arrived at a full-functioning airport. As was customary in those days, the controller on the ground would flash a green light if conditions were favorable to land or a red light if we were to go around the traffic pattern again until given the green light. It was, believe me, nothing like it is today. But the excitement of it was unmistakable. Rollin and I were two happy larks.

We traveled east to McCook, Nebraska, where the favorable bright, sunny weather was changing to heavy, dark storm clouds. Rain was imminent. With no radio or instruments, there was no way we could continue to fly in the inclement weather. We were able to make a landing at a small airport and spent the evening in a

31

nearby motel. It was a long four days before we could take off again. But sometimes things do happen for the best. Rollin and I did enjoy some pleasurable, loving moments. We often wondered if this new love of flying we both had also affected our libido, for we were in great form! We also learned another flying lesson. When planning a trip by air, make sure you have plenty of time to spare for, indeed, weather can halt everything.

The time we spent in this little town was also extra memorable for us, not only because of the time we had together, but because we were able to really concentrate more on our flying maps and new innovations (at least in that day and age).

We eventually found ourselves approaching Kansas City and were just mesmerized by all the airplanes in the sky. (In those days several planes was big stuff.) We were used to seeing maybe one or two in the areas where we had flown. The sight of so many frightened us, and we decided that we would definitely try to avoid large cities. Our trip was planned around visiting towns in Kansas, Ohio, and Iowa seeing relatives along the way. Taking some of them for their first ride was a really big event not only for them but for us as we "politely" showed off our new skills.

One of the dangers of flying in those days was starving to death as there were no restaurants, no food machines, no food vendors of any sort at the airports. However, there was comradeship between airport owners and pilots who landed. Often some would loan us their car to go into town or invite us to their homes. Courtesy was a very big thing, and we would later find ourselves doing the same when we owned our own flying service.

We were flying over a large cornfield, approaching a landing strip in Iowa. Upon landing, we were informed that the farmer did not mind the pilots landing around his cornfield and never complained about the low flying aircraft. A group of us pilots decided to purchase some of the corn and arrange for a corn roast and goodies one evening. Flying stories were exchanged and many of us bragged about this aircraft or that but especially about our flying conquests. It was a different way of life. Gatherings such as this were known among the pilots as "hangar flying."

Alcohol was illegal in some of the states, particularly in the Midwest. However, the motel/hotel owners always had available the name of a local bootlegger in the event some pilots were hanging in for a spell and needed a relaxing drink before the evening meal. Nothing like the big Chicago bootlegging days, though.

Our next stop was South Bend, Indiana, where we visited and walked around the Notre Dame University campus. Though we had no Irish connections, we enjoyed the fans of the Fighting Irish football team. We later found ourselves to become fans because of those memories.

Flying over the Allegheny Mountains was much more challenging than we had expected. After making it over the Colorado mountains, you'd think going over the eastern mountains would be a piece of cake, but it wasn't. There are fifty-three majestic mountain peaks with an elevation of fourteen thousand feet or more in Colorado. We could simply determine our flight destination over those mountains with reference to a mountain peak, making navigation easy.

The Allegheny Mountains, however, were completely covered with tall trees so that roads and railroad tracks were not visible to us. We became rather disoriented, making turns to the right and then left in an effort to locate a reference point. Perhaps, we had acquired some of the "luck of the Irish" from South Bend, Indiana, because we finally saw a small airport in a clearing beneath us and immediately started our approach. The runway was short and surrounded by trees. We had to make several attempts before we could land and wondered how on earth other planes managed to land there!

Most of our experience in takeoffs and landings had been at an altitude of sixty-two hundred feet, and we had to keep a reasonable air speed on landings so as not to stall the plane before reaching the ground. We didn't realize that the heavier and more stable air at lower altitudes would allow a plane to land at a slower speed. We finally figured out that we could make our approach over the top of the trees and slow the plane enough to make a safe landing. This was one landing we were happy to have completed and climbed out very tired and hungry.

Our first question to the airport manager was, "Where is the nearest place to eat?" We were told that a lady who lived nearby served breakfast in her home. We borrowed his car and made our way to the top of one of the smaller mountains and walked into the dining room. It was a memorable greeting. A lovely lady wearing a dark blue cotton dress covered with a bright white apron approached us. As she seated us near one of the windows we were taken aback by the spectacular mountains and views. It was a sight, even today, I have not forgotten along with the wonderful hospitality of that time. It was as if were were good friends or neighbors who had just stopped in. Our breakfast was fantastic with fresh eggs, blueberries, and all those homemade goodies of the day. When Rollin went to pay he was told the price was $1.50 and he remonstrated saying, "Lady, you can't serve such a wonderful meal for just $1.50!"

She simply replied, "I think that you misunderstood me. It is seventy-five cents EACH—$1.50 is the total."

Rollin tried to slip a five-dollar bill under a plate on the table, but she was aware and promptly handed the money back saying, "No tipping allowed."

We thanked her and took one last look at the view and realized that in some way all that beauty was so highly reflected in this wonderful hostess.

Since we had already decided that air traffic in New York City would present too much of a challenge, we made plans to head for New Jersey. We decided we could take a train into the city later. We were able to book into the Waldorf Astoria and managed to see a Broadway show that evening. The next day we made plans to enjoy a baseball game at Yankee Stadium. We were taken aback while at the stadium when suddenly we heard, "Hey, Sono." We looked around only to see a friend that Rollin had attended school with in Florence, Colorado. Talk about small worlds! He was with his wife and daughter and sitting not far from us in the stadium. Now seeing someone WE knew right there in N.Y.C. so far from Colorado was a big treat for us. We were so exuberant and noisy, we attracted a lot of attention but especially a gentleman sitting nearby, who turned out to be Walter Winchell, the ace reporter of the day. He was very outgoing and impressed with our enthusiasm. We were pleasantly surprised to find that he mentioned us in his radio broadcast the next Sunday after he greeted, "Mr. and Mrs. America and all the ships at sea," which was the manner he used in opening his radio broadcast. We felt very, very important!

We were taken in by the profusion of lakes, rivulets, vegetation, and the variety of scenery throughout New England. It was beautiful and different. We landed at North Grafton Airport and were met by some family and friends. All were eager for an airplane flight, and we enjoyed, once again, showing off our great flying talents.

Flying Joyfully

New England did have a lot of meaning. When I was eighteen years old, as a graduation present, my parents gave me a trip back to Worcester, Massachusetts, to visit my mother's relatives there. I fell in love with the beautiful, peaceful, New England area. I loved to swim in the lakes and enjoyed the beautiful sky and fluffy clouds. We did not have quite the same view in Colorado. It brought back a deep closeness to my family and the many friends I made in the area. Rollin soon learned why I had fallen in love with New England. We enjoyed our visit there, paddled a canoe, did fun things with the family, but were kept busy giving plane rides!

It was time for us to begin our return flight. Now that we were braver and more experienced, we no longer avoided the large cities and planned our itinerary so that we would land at different airports on our return trip. It was a long flight with the route we had planned—eleven hundred miles from Quincy, Illinois, to Florence, Colorado, where we visited Rollin's parents for a few days. They were jubilant at our arrival and excited to hear all the news about our flying and activities. From Florence, Colorado, we flew across the mountains back to Cortez. After being gone a month, Cortez did look beautiful to us, and we longed to be home again. Our landing strip was no landing strip. It was full of weeds and sunflowers. No one had maintained the airport, and thinking that perhaps we would not return with our airplane, it had been neglected. Rollin carefully maneuvered a landing through the weeds without any damage to the aircraft. It was our FIRST flying adventure, and we had made it cross country and back safely. We had traveled from Colorado to the East Coast and returned without having to stop for a red light or maneuver through highway traffic! There would be, however, many more trips to come.

HOBBY TURNS INTO A BUSINESS

We couldn't believe how many of our friends and others in the area wanted to learn fly. Not too long ago, there was a certain negativity throughout the country that this "flying thing" would not last. How little we knew then. Just take a look at the busy skies today not to mention airports all over the place!

I had been taking passengers up for a ride almost every day after I had gotten my pilot's license, which entitled me to take passengers, BUT not for hire. As my first passenger, I took a very close friend up for a ride. I was personally excited but also realized the gravity of the situation—I would be responsible for the safety not only of myself but my friend and passenger, not to mention the aircraft! It turned out to be a fun flight with no incident and later that day at a luncheon, the group was fascinated with the idea of my close friend being my first passenger. But one young lady in the group announced, "Oh my, Polly, I would not want to be the first passenger,"

I smiled and replied, "Well, look at it this way; it's better to be the first than the last." We had some laughs over that. Today, my friend is now a healthy, lovely lady in her nineties. To this day the greeting words between us are: "It's better to be the first than the last."

Shortly after, I decided to try for my Instructor's Rating so I could teach interested students to become pilots. Because of my own experiences, it was extra important to me that students learn to become good, safe pilots. To my knowledge, none of my students who later became pilots were ever injured flying their own planes.

Rollin and I worked hard toward acquiring our two hundred hours of solo flight time. Eventually, we completed the solo and passed our written exam for flight instructor's rating. Now, we were ready to train anyone that wanted to learn to fly. Our hobby had turned into a business. I ran the flight school while Rollin worked at the bank until closing time at 3 p.m. He would come to the field, and we would continue to fly and train until dark. Because we only had one car, I used my bicycle to get to the airport every morning—a good two mile ride. But at least I did not have to ride it back home—we just put it into the trunk of the car. As much as I did not mind riding a bicycle, it was only transportation to get back into the air where I wanted to be.

My father was very impressed with our ingenuity and our new flying business. He built us another home on a little hill on the airport property with a small guest house. Rollin and I realized just how lucky we were. We had come a long way and made sacrifices to get where we were, but we were blessed with Father's help.

So there I was, at the airport almost twenty-four hours a day. I would get up at dawn to give flying lessons and walk back up the hill at dusk to prepare a light dinner for Rollin and myself. We would go to bed exhausted some nights but happier than we could have ever imagined. Teaching others to fly and being with friends who had the same love of flying was very rewarding. And the best part was we were doing something we loved doing.

We seldom drove our car except into town for necessities. We simply flew to the nearby towns and cities. We had now acquired several small planes for instruction use. Occasionally Rollin and I would fly different planes to the same destination to see who could get there first. Our most frequently visited airport was nearby Farmington, New Mexico. We had many friends there whom we enjoyed. They were aware of the friendly competition between Rollin and me. One day when we were in the flight pattern, the Farmington Airport owner's five-year-old son was heard saying, "Hey, Daddy, Polly's going to win today."

Our own airport lounge was a gathering place for those who loved to fly. If we were not flying, you could find us and our flying buddies sitting around talking flying—"hangar flying."

Early one Sunday evening a group of us were all dressed up, planning to go to a nice restaurant for dinner. As we started out, someone noticed smoke over the town, "There must be a fire, let's check it out." We all jumped into our own little planes and took off. A lady friend was in with me, her husband was Rollin's passenger. It was a lovely summer evening, and I was flying about three hundred feet over the town, when there was a loud noise, and the engine in my aircraft quit. The crankshaft had broken. I calmly made a ninety-degree turn, and the only place I could see that might be suitable for a landing was a small vacant lot, surrounded by high tension wires. I headed for it, was able to pull the plane up over the wires, and landed safely in the field without damage to the aircraft or ourselves.

However, there were high weeds in the field, and we had on our nicest clothes including silk hosiery, which were difficult to obtain during the World War II years, so we decided to take them off before getting out of the plane. When people came rushing to the plane to see if we were still alive, we were calmly sitting there taking off our silk stockings.

My passenger remained calm throughout the experience, and later I heard her telling friends, "Polly was magnificent. I wasn't frightened at all as she was completely in charge of the situation, and soon we were safely on the ground."

This was my first forced landing in a plane where the engine quit and I had to land the plane without power. There were to be two more in my career.

As a flight instuctor, I had my share of challenging students. Three were especially memorable.

One was the insurance salesman: Each of my students was different in his or her ability to learn to fly. This gentleman from a nearby town required fifty additional hours of flight training before he could finally be trusted to go alone. He was determined and dedicated to get his license. Most students required eight to ten hours of dual flight. When he finally made his solo flight, there was a huge crowd at the airport to cheer him.

Another was the young boy student: This young lad just could not bring himself to look out the plane window. When I insisted that he had to know what was going on all around him not just through the front window, he would look under the seat instead of out the windows. He probably would have made a great instrument pilot having this sort of "window phobia." We did not have instruments in our plane at that time. Eventually he was able to cope. At times—although it was many years ago—I wonder where and how he is today.

And then there was the prominent Cortez Lady: This woman was indeed well-known but not very sports minded, so it surprised me when she told me she wanted to learn to fly. I knew I could teach her. After many hours in the air and practicing takeoffs and landings, I decided that she just wasn't going to get any better. So early one morning, I let her take the plane up for her solo flight. At her first attempt at landing she hit the ground and bounced up twenty feet in the air. I had always taught my students that if they made a bad landing to gun the engine of the airplane and go around the flight pattern and try again. She did this FIVE times, bouncing high every time. The mechanics and others on the ground were all frantic as they watched. I was confident, however, that she could make it. On the sixth try, she finally made a perfectly smooth three point landing. I don't think she actually flew very much after that, but she did solo and made sure the townspeople knew it. Personally, I knew she could do it.

Student pilots all have a different feel about flying. Some are just natural—some require a lot more experience. Just a few years ago I heard that she was celebrating her ninetieth birthday at a retirement home in Albuquerque, New Mexico, so I sent a card and a note. She wrote back, and I still have her letter where she wrote: "Polly, I shall never forget the big smile on your face when I landed after my first solo flight". In thinking back, of course I was pleased with her finally making the perfect landing, but I was very happy to get my student and my plane back safely on the ground with no damage to either one.

CONTINUING TALES OF FLYING

Our flying was not limited to flight instruction only, as the Four Corners area is a most fascinating part of the United States. Monument Valley was only a thirty minute flight from our airport in Cortez, so whenever we had time, we headed there. For those who have never visited Monument Valley, do so. The scenery is magnificent and offers inspiration.

Mike and Harry Goulding owned the Monument Valley Lodge and Trading Post. Harry had been in the sheep raising business near Durango, Colorado, and as all ranchers did, he would take his sheep into the warmer areas of Utah for the winter months. When he first saw the spectacular formations of Monument Valley, he went home to Durango to tell his bride-to-be, "Mike" as she was called, that he had found the place where they were to live. Mike's real name was Leona, but Harry thought that was too difficult to pronounce, so he had personally "baptized her" as Mike and the rest of us joined in.

After their marriage and move to Monument Valley, which was on the Navajo Indian Reservation, they lived in a tent until they could build the trading post. Here natives could purchase supplies. Mike and Harry had their living quarters above the store, which consisted of a living room, kitchen, two bedrooms, and a bathroom.

Eventually, a few guest cottages were built. Because they did not have a water well at that time, they had to haul it in. There was only a pitcher for water and a small bowl for guests to use as a body washing facility. And, of course, there was the out-house toilet. One did not visit there for the comforts of home but rather to enjoy the magnificent scenery and the wonderful people who came there.

They had a small airstrip where we could land the plane uphill and take off downhill which took some skill. Many of the students were nearing acquisition of their private pilot's license. I got a kick out of taking some of these students there to see if they could negotiate a landing on this airstrip. My husband, however, who was a bold pilot, enjoyed announcing his arrival by flying low and up the canyon over the trading post which was against a cliff. Believe me, it took careful, alert flying. I never have been a bold pilot.

One day as usual, we both flew our own plane, and when I landed, Rollin was standing beside his plane. His face was white as a sheet. "Polly," he said, "I hit a down draft and just knocked off the top of the chimney of the Goulding house."

Harry arrived at the field to pick us up and walked over to Rollin and said, "Ok, you have been trying to do that for a long time. Now that you have accomplished it, you needn't try it again."

We drove up the hill to their home, and I went inside to help Mike clean up the soot in her living room. It was a very small price to pay when we might have been picking up airplane pieces instead, not to mention, what could have happened to Rollin! Luckily there was no damage to the wing. Mike told me what a shock it was to her when she heard this loud thump and then saw ashes coming down the chimney into the living room.

MONUMENT VALLEY—
FILMING THE MOVIES

Times were difficult for the Navajos on the reservation, so Harry decided to go to Hollywood to see if he could entice a movie company to come to Monument Valley to film a picture. Perhaps they could hire some of the Indians so they would have an income.

He and Mike drove to Hollywood. Harry was a tall lanky cowboy type. He could make a sort of grand entrance. So there he was, walking into the office of Samuel Goldwyn of the Goldwyn/Mayer Studio, with pictures of Monument Valley. He could be an amazing salesman. Before he left, he had a check in his hand to purchase groceries and supplies along with orders to be prepared for a movie crew to arrive within a week. We had the unique experience of being present to see the creation of several of the countless movies filmed in Monument Valley. Early Westerns were big in those days. It was exciting for all of us as we became acquainted with actors and crew.

John Ford was the director of the first movie filming we witnessed. He was teaching handsome John Wayne how to act. Once while I was watching, John Wayne rode his horse to the top of a hill and looked down at the director and said, "What do I do now?" John Ford replied, "Smile," and the big John Wayne smile that appeared still remains in my memory today.

The film crew also depended on Harry to tell them where the best views would be. Although the Monument Valley had been their home for years, Harry would readily admit that every day was a new revelation to him in viewing the valley. He would say, as the clouds and light changed, "Now just look at that. Isn't that breath-taking?"

When I took Harry up in the plane with his camera, he would see something he wanted to photograph and say to me, "Ok Polly, bend it," meaning the airplane, then, "Bend it the other way, gal." So I was twisting and turning all over the sky in order for him to get just the picture he wanted. It was great fun. In thinking back I realize just much fun I REALLY did have. Later, Harry would put up a screen and show the pictures to the guests in the lodge. They were spectacular. I firmly believe that a person, such as Harry, had to have this deep love of the valley to get such perfect views. He instinctively knew just how and where to get the great shots.

Evenings in Monument Valley were filled with laughter and fun especially while they were filming movies. One night the female Indians put on a Squaw Dance. In their colorful costumes, they danced around a large circle and would pick a man from the audience, hold on to his belt and force him to dance until he gave her some money. One squaw picked out Henry Fonda for her partner and they danced and danced and danced because he did not have any money in his pocket. He was getting tired and pleaded to his friends to go up to his room and get some money for him. We were all enjoying his plight and his pleading, but eventually one of them relented and went to get him some money. He gave him a quarter, which Henry Fonda handed to the squaw who then released him.

Many of the people from the production group wanted to take plane rides over the valley just to view it from the air. They would locate places for filming and this was a privilege I truly delighted in. How can anyone forget being around a filming crew—especially in those days. I'll never forget the big broad shoulders of John Wayne as he sat alongside me in that small aircraft. He was a big but gentle person, and I enjoyed his exuberant remarks as he viewed the red rock monuments from above. Meeting actors and movie people was an experience I never would have expected in my life. What a thrill!

CONTINUING STORIES OF
THE FAMOUS AND NOT-SO-FAMOUS

Mike did all the cooking on a small coal stove. She was a wonderful cook and prepared fabulous meals and homemade bread that melted in your mouth. Oftentimes if Rollin happened to be in the area, he would stop just to see if Mike had an extra loaf of bread he could bring back home to me. The happy meals and conversations were special moments. I realize today how few families or friends spend any time sitting around a table, enjoying some good food and conversations.

Mike's mother and Aunt Molly lived with them at this point. They both had cheerful dispositions and were great fun. Coincidentally, we happened to be there visiting on December 7,

1941 when we were told that the Japanese had bombed Pearl Harbor. To say we were stunned would be an understatement. We just could not believe what we were hearing! Those hours we spent together going over and over how this sort of thing could happen have remained in my mind to this day.

When World War II ended, we made a point of going back there so all of us could celebrate. I recall when we landed, Aunt Molly was out on the porch waving a large white sheet. Upon landing, Molly popped off the cork of a bottle of champagne, and we toasted to "Thank God, peace again."

Meanwhile, Jimmy and Gretchen Swinnerton arrived to join the celebration. Jimmy was the famous cartoonist of "The Canyon Kiddies" published in the Hearst newspapers. He was a very talented artist as well. My home contains original paintings that he did of Monument Valley, Ship Rock, New Mexico, and the California desert. He also drew a cartoon of me, which I have in my logbook. It shows my plane flying above the clouds with Jimmy, the Canyon Kiddie, with his dog beside him, waving at the plane and saying, "Good luck." It is a special treasure of mine.

Another unforgettable excursion to Monument Valley started in Cortez one evening when we were getting ready to close flight operations for the day. Harry Combs and his wife, Clare, friends of ours from Denver, flew in and suggested that we fly down to the valley for the night.

We were to have a house guest, Leila Fulton, a lady we had met some time ago in Monument Valley, along with her husband. Rollin was to fly her to Albuquerque the next day on a charter trip. Because we knew she loved the valley as much as we did, we asked her to fly with us and spend the night. Rollin could take her on to Albuquerque the next morning, and I could simply fly back to Cortez to start giving my early morning lessons. She agreed and off we went. I had been to the grocery store that morning and had a loaf of bread in the car which, on the spur of the moment, I threw into the luggage compartment of the plane, although I could not imagine anyone taking a loaf of store-bought bread into Mike Goulding's kitchen!

When our three planes landed at the trading post, no one came to pick us up, and it was quite evident that the place was deserted. By this time the sun was setting, and it was too late for us to head back home. There was nothing to do but walk up the hill to the trading post to see if we could find a place to sleep. An Indian outside the building told us the Gouldings had gone to Flagstaff for the week.

Rollin and Harry Combs found a ladder and climbed to the upstairs porch. They removed a screen and opened a window to get into the bedroom. They proceeded to get downstairs and opened the door for Leila, Clare, and myself. Mike's refrigerator was completely empty. We looked through the shelves and found a few cans of beef stew and soup.

There were two bedrooms. One contained a full-size double bed, and the other, which Rollin and I had slept in before, had two twin beds. When it came time to retire there were some decisions to be made. It was agreed that Harry and Clare would have the bedroom with the double bed, and Rollin and I would sleep together, in one of the twin beds while Leila took the other twin bed. It worked out quite well although it was a "chummy close night."

I awakened and went to see if I could get something for breakfast. Only that loaf of bread I had brought along was available with some canned fruit. We made the beds, cleaned up a bit, and left a note explaining what we had done and promised when we returned we would not "break and enter" again. Rollin and Leila took off for

Albuquerque while Harry and Clare headed to Denver and I flew back to Cortez. It was another Monument Valley adventure.

Several weeks later, Rollin and I happened to be at the lodge in Monument Valley at the same time Leila and her husband were there. Her husband had some business to take care of in Mexican Hat, Utah, not too far away, where there was a small airstrip. He asked me to fly him there the next morning which I agreed to do. We took off early in the morning and when we returned to the trading post, the rest of the group was sitting around eating breakfast. Leila said kiddingly, "Polly, I don't know what to think of you taking off at the crack of dawn with my husband."

I replied, "Now, Leila, did I say anything when you slept all night with my husband?" and then I turned and walked into the kitchen.

Everyone started to laugh, and Leila called to me, "Polly, you have to come back and explain that one." I just laughed and let her do her own explaining. I relate this incident as I do others in my story simply to show the happy camaraderie that existed between us.

Harry Combs later sold his flight operation in Denver and became president of Lear Jet, then upon retirement, moved to western Colorado then on to Arizona. A friend told me that he had mentioned my name in one of the books he had written. My daughter found his phone number on the Internet so that I was able to call him. We reminisced about earlier times, and I asked him if he remember our break-and-enter flight into Monument Valley. He said, "Polly, how could I ever forget that?"

SOME HAPPY AND NOT-SO-HAPPY ADVENTURES

One day I was in Monument Valley by myself. I often would fly in supplies, and if Harry wanted to make a bank deposit, he would put the money in a paper sack, and I would take it back home with me. I would hide it in my washing machine until Rollin could take it to the bank the next day. On this particular flight, my airplane was securely tied down on the airstrip, and I was in the trading post talking to Harry, when a Navajo came running in saying, "Bird upside down." We rushed to the window to look out, and there was my plane, lying upside down. A whirlwind had come along, causing the stakes to pull up, flipping the plane over. Well, now this was my favorite plane, Pansy, so I started to cry as I stood there looking at it.

I think Harry felt as badly as I did and offered to drive me to Cortez so I could make arrangements for the plane to be repaired. As we drove past the airport at Mexican Hat, Utah, we noticed that something was wrong. Norman Neville, who had a business of taking tourists down the river in boats to the Natural Bridges Monument (a fun and interesting trip), also had a plane there. He was very well known. That morning he and his wife had taken off in their plane, and shortly after, the engine quit. He made an abrupt turn in an effort to get back to the airport, but the plane stalled out and crashed. They both lost their lives. This, indeed, made my plane incident seem like nothing.

It did not take long for our airplane mechanic to get the spare parts needed to repair my plane, and once again, Pansy and I were flying together.

Wabbit Twacks

TRAINING STUDENTS
AND ADVENTURES

I loved taking off in our own planes, traveling on the spur of the moment or planning trips in advance. But my true passion was training students to fly. Each one was so different in his or her reactions and reasons for wanting to fly.

I accepted the responsibility of their safety and did not overlook any actions that might cause them to get into trouble when they flew alone. I wanted them to feel the movements of the plane and its capabilities, to know the weather and when it was not safe to fly, to feel the air currents, and to observe where they might expect downdrafts and updrafts. Because the air is thin flying at high altitudes in Colorado, it was necessary for the student to know this and be able to cope with the changes. Dedication and patience were big requirements.

I spent many hours with each student, practicing take-offs and landings, stalls, spins, and other maneuvers, but always at an altitude that allowed me to get the plane back to the airport if the engine should quit, which it did on a couple of occasions.

One day when one of my male students was performing a three-turn spin for me, he froze on the controls and did not level off after the spins were completed. Here we were with the nose of the plane straight down, headed for the ground at high speed. He was a strong fellow, and I realized I couldn't take over the controls from him, so I calmly tapped him on the shoulder and said, "It's time to ease back on the stick now." After the third time, my voice still calm and persuasive, he relaxed and brought the plane back to level flight. I think I was trembling somewhat when I complimented him on his maneuver and suggested we go back to the airport. I'm not sure he ever realized just how close we had been to disaster.

One of my most dedicated female students loved learning to fly, and I spent a lot of dual time with her. Upon landing one day, she got too close to the weeds next to the runway, and before I could make a correction, one of the wheels caught the growth, and the plane slowly and gently went over on its nose. Fortunately, I had managed to quickly turn off the engine, and the propeller was not damaged. I told her not to unfasten the seat belt too quickly, or she would fall on her head. By using caution, we were able to crawl out of the plane safely.

Later she purchased her own plane which she named "Wabbit Twacks," and she loved that plane as if it were a child. Unfortunately, Wabbit Twacks came to its end one day a few years later when it caught on fire as she was flying over the mountains in Denver. She was able to land the plane in a clearing, and both she and her passenger quickly got out of the plane, ran into the woods, and escaped without injury. They were rescued by a forest ranger, but Wabbit Twacks was no more.

Recollections, submitted by Duain Caylor

My first recollection of flying in Southwest Colorado began in 1937, when a strip of sage brush just east of Cortez was cleared for a landing strip. A 40 HP Piper Cub plane appeared and began taking people for rides around the valley for $2.00 each. I did **not** get a ride.

In September 1944, I took my first two lessons with Polly Usher as my instuctor, flying a 65 hp Taylorcraft. From April through September 1945 I took another eight and a quarter hours of instruction in the T craft.

In June 1946 Polly switched planes on me to a 65 HP J-3 Piper Cub, and I took my first solo flight on June 19, 1946. I was a little frightened.

I completed my training and flight test on July 16, 1947. I have never flown solo since.

Ben Caylor, a second cousin took instuction also in 1947 and purchased his own aircraft in which his sixteen-year-old daughter soloed on the day that Monarch airlines made their debut at the Cortez airport.

P.S. Polly's husband, Rollin, instructed me on one occasion in some aerobatics that Polly refused to instruct me in. She was a safety conscious instructor. Many thanks to the Ushers for promoting air advancements in the four corners area.

When I was alone at the airport, I would take a plane and go up in the air just to practice and "fly joyfully." I would do spins, stalls, chandelles, loops, and whatever maneuvers the plane was capable of performing, or just fly along the mesa, feeling the updrafts and downdrafts. These were such special pleasurable moments and still today, at eighty-nine years of age, those "flying joyfully" episodes are dear to my heart.

One day I noticed what appeared to be six straight trees in a row near the top of the mesa. It looked rather unusual for six trees to be in a line like that, so I flew closer to investigate. What I saw were not trees at all, but six openings into an ancient cliff dwelling. The main Mesa Verde cliff dwellings were miles away, so I thought, perhaps this is a small dwelling that had not yet been discovered. I was quite excited as I flew back to the airport, and the experience remained in my thoughts for the rest of the evening. The next day my sister Evelyn and her husband Harry came from Denver to visit. When I told them of my finding, they suggested that we hike up there to investigate more closely. We had visions in our heads of finding a ruin that had not been seen since the ancient cliff dwellers had left it and, perhaps, finding some of their beautiful pottery.

I was eager to go. We took some water along with us and drove our car as close as we could get, then started hiking up the mesa. We came upon a trail that eventually led us to the cliff dwelling. Our hopes of being the first explores were dashed when we found an empty cigarette package in the first doorway. There was no visible pottery in sight, and we did not want to destroy any of the ancient ruins by digging inside. However, what a thrill it was just to sit there and imagine the life of the cliff dwellers. Did they ever think that some day a "huge bird" that had an engine and propeller might observe their home? The view from this spot was spectacular, looking out into the valley and seeing Ute Mountain.

Ute Mountain is located west of our airport and resembles an Indian stretched out approximately eight miles. The northern end looks like the head of an Indian with a feathered headdress. The high part of the mountain, his chest, flows on south into the legs, knees, and finally, a rock standing at the end: his toes. One can imagine the delightful time God must have had in creating the striking landmark right on the Indian reservation. It is sacred and respected by all the Indians and is a landmark for all pilots.

We picked up the empty cigarette pack and hiked down the trail to our car. We were a little disappointed that we had not made a first discovery but pleased, anyway, with the adventure.

I had interaction with the Ute Indians, whose reservation was south of our airport, as they had a curiosity about airplanes and had built a small airstrip at Ship Rock, New Mexico. Ship Rock was another landmark of the valley—a huge rock resembling a sailing ship, which can be seen for miles in all directions. Here they would have Indian Fairs and celebrations. I would fly down for the one day and take up passengers for three dollars a ride. I would be busy all day taking up passengers, one after another. They were all so eager to go up in the plane. I enjoyed seeing the big smiles on their faces while they were in the air and observing everything on the ground, but it was a hectic day for me because the large crowd did not always realize the danger of getting near the plane. While I was landing, some of the on-lookers would blissfully run with their dogs across the runway right in front of my plane. So the minute I landed, I had to apply the brakes to stop as quickly as possible. There was a brake for each wheel located just next to the rudder pedals. I had to brace myself to press hard on the brakes with my heels while still controlling the direction of the plane. When I arrived back home in the evening, I would have a large painful welt extending across my back from the constant pressure, along with aching muscles in all parts of my body. I really didn't volunteer for this venture very often.

The interest in flying soon became far beyond our expectations. The main farming crop in the region was pinto beans. My husband, Rollin, being the astute banker that he was, would loan money for the growth of the crops. The proceeds from the farms soon expanded, and many of the farmers were buying their own planes, and eventually, the wives wanted me to teach them to fly also.

Soon, in this town of two thousand people, there were twenty-two privately owned airplanes, five of which belonged to us. We purchased the planes we needed from the Combs and Hayden Airport in Denver. It became my responsibility to go there to pick them up since it seems that I was the only one who had the patience to fly over the fourteen-thousand-foot mountains to bring the planes back to Cortez.

It took a lot of time to get the sixty-five-horsepower plane to an altitude high enough to cross the mountains, and often when you arrived at the mountain pass, there would be a strong head wind, and the plane would barely move forward. It might take an hour before I could get through Wolf Creek Pass, and then I would barely make it to the airport in Alamosa to refuel so that I could continue the two-hour flight home. If the wind was too strong, I would have to turn back to refuel at the nearest town, then try again. When I would finally return home after one of these trips, I would have flu-like symptoms and spend the rest of the day resting in bed. It wasn't until some time later that I realized that being at such a high altitude without oxygen was causing my problem.

The town of Cortez was supposed to maintain the land next to our airport. However, because most of the taxpayers did not want to make any outlay for the upkeep, it was not in good shape. Rollin and I could see the future of aviation in the area so Rollin asked the town to sell the land to us, and we would make the needed improvements. At a special meeting of the Town Board, it was agreed upon.

The work was completed and it was not too long before Frontier Airlines started regularly scheduled service into Cortez from Denver, Salt Lake City, and Phoenix. This was a great moment in our lives and we have been commended for our efforts in building up both private and commercial aviation in the southwest part of Colorado.

Besides flying, I took part in the volunteer activities of the town, and at one time served as President of the St. Barnabas Church Women's Auxiliary. After a visit from the Diocesan President from Denver, Mrs. Clarence Moore, she reported that her visit to the Western Slope Missions was inspirational and praised the capable work of Mrs. Polly Usher, President of the St. Barnabas Guild and added, "Mr. & Mrs. Usher own their own planes in which they tour about the United States. I would not be surprised if she was the only Auxiliary President in the American Church who flies an airplane." My volunteer work was enjoyable because I did meet so many people who were not only interesting but also interested in me.

Soon the twenty-two airplanes in the area climbed to twenty-five privately owned aircraft. As a result we started the Ute Flying Club, which would later became well known throughout the state.

Every Sunday morning we would take off as a group and fly someplace for breakfast, eating at restaurants and lodges, or often taking along our own food and cooking outdoors. Over the years we visited many airports in Colorado, Arizona, New Mexico and Utah.

One of the ladies I taught to fly and who had her own airplane, was always getting lost. The rest of us would all have been on the ground for a half-hour or more, and here she would come from a different direction altogether. I don't know how she did it, but she always showed up. We would spend some anxious moments waiting, but then someone would cry out, "Here she comes," and we would all relax. When we weren't flying out of town, we would have cookouts at our own airport, and we would have some contests:

- Spot Landing Contests to see who could touch down closest to a designated spot. I am happy to say my women students always won this contest.
- Toilet paper contests where each participant would take off with a roll of toilet paper, go to an altitude of five hundred feet, toss the roll out then see how many times they could cut through it before it reached the ground. The men pilots performed best at this challenge.

It might seem that this last contest might be a dangerous maneuver, but we were all good pilots, and no one was ever in trouble. The next day, however, people wondered about all the toilet paper gracefully draped over the sagebrush around the airport.

The following is a little jingle I wrote about the spot landing contests:

A Spot Landing Contest was the order of the day
The losers had to cook the food while the winners could just play
So each one took an airplane, with a couple to keep books.
They missed the spot both far and wide. We did not lack for cooks.

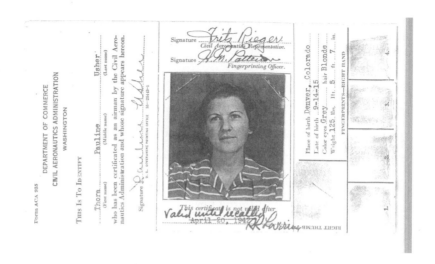

Form ACA 935

DEPARTMENT OF COMMERCE
CIVIL AERONAUTICS ADMINISTRATION
WASHINGTON

THIS IS TO IDENTIFY

Thora   Pauline   Usher
(First name)   (Middle name)   (Last name)

who has been certificated as an airman by the Civil Aeronautics Administration and whose signature appears hereon.

Signature ....

Signature _____
          Civil Aeronautics Representative.
Signature _____
          Fingerprinting Officer.

Place of birth Denver, Colorado
Date of birth 9-14-15
Color eyes Grey   hair Blonde
Weight 125 lbs. Ht. 5   ft. 7   in.

FINGERPRINTS—RIGHT HAND

This certificate is not valid after
April 20, 1942

Valid until recalled

RIGHT THUMB

UNCLE SAM CALLS

World War II came along, and then the fun was over. A Civil Aeronautics inspector came to Cortez from Denver and explained that our country was ill prepared to fight a war and asked if we would participate in a Civil Pilots Training Program. The program would take qualified people in our area and give them their basic ground and flight training, and from there they would be taken into the Air Force. We, of course, were excited to be part of such a project.

The flight examiner also asked me if I would try for a Civil Aeronautics Examiner's rating so that I would also be able to issue licenses. So, again, I was up before dawn every morning to study meteorolgy, navigation, and rules and regulations so that I could start a ground school along with the flight school. Because of my experience in instruction, I passed the flight test with flying colors and became one of the very few Female Flight Examiners in the country.

One of the requirements for having a government flight school was that we have a gun on the premises as a precaution should an enemy plane land there. We purchased an old German Luger pistol and placed it in the back of one of our filing cabinets, feeling pretty sure that we would never have use for it.

We now needed additional employees to handle the enlargement of the flying service. An instructor from Farmington, New Mexico, and one from Mancos, Colorado, a small town near Cortez, came to help us out. I also hired a small, young man who was a competent flight instructor from Utah, named Fank Brgoch. I depended on him a lot and when he wasn't busy giving flight instructions, I would send him to deliver planes to another school we had started in Blanding, Utah, and on charter trips also. As qualified as he was, he was sometimes a worry to me because occasionally he would return from a trip a couple of hours later than I had expected him. His explanation was that he had become tired and decided to take a nap before returning. That particular behavior was very easy for him and it became—I believe—an important survival tactic during WWII.

I told Frank that I was going to quit worrying about him. If an engine quit on the plane he was flying and he was forced to land somewhere in a deserted area, he would just have to start walking because I would not be looking for him. Later, he DID have that happen to him on a return flight from Monument Valley. His first thought after landing the plane was, "Well, I'd better start walking because Polly won't be looking for me." He walked several miles back to the trading post and phoned me from there. I sent a plane to bring him home, and a mechanic to repair the engine. When he returned he had a rather sheepish grin on his face. After that he made an effort to keep me advised as to where he was and when he would return.

We hired two more mechanics and a young transient boy who came by looking for a job. He was of Polish descent—John Tschkowski was his name. He was a good worker, handsome, pleasant, and a fun person. Since he didn't have a place to stay, we let him sleep in the small guest house we had on our property. I felt like an older sister to him, and we were always joking with each other. One day while we were talking, I saw a small pretty, pink rock lying on the ground. I picked it up and handed it to him and he put it in his pocket. A few days later, I found it placed underneath my logbook. The following week I went up to his room while he was away and laid it on his pillow. This little contest went on for months, each one challenged to find a new location for the rock so the other one would be sure to find it. One day I was away on a charter trip, reached into my pocket for something, and there was the rock! How it got there without my knowledge was a mystery to me. The game was fun until one day he placed it in an envelope, addressed it to me, and sent it by mail. When I took the envelope out of the mailbox, it had only a hole in it and the rock was gone. John was disappointed when I told him it had not survived the postal service.

John's social life was running into problems at this time. He had fallen in love with a girl who belonged to a strange religious cult that had recently come into town. What went on, I do not know, but his personality changed from a fun-loving young man, to an unhappy, despondent person. One morning he did not show up for work, but his car was outside of the guest house. Thinking, perhaps, he had been out late and had overslept, I didn't do anything about it for a couple of hours. Later I became concerned and went up to his room only to discover that he had not slept in his bed the previous night. I sent several people into town to see if they could find him. As the day went on, and he hadn't been located, we all became very worried. Finally, Rollin got into a plane to fly low over the area. He soon returned, got out of the airplane quickly and came over to tell me that Johnny's body was lying in the weeds in a field not far from the airport. I was in complete shock and ran screaming, "No, no, no!" into the airport office, and looked behind the filing cabinet to find that the Luger was missing. What a sad loss of a beautiful life. I notified his family in Oklahoma. They had the body sent there and we were never to know why such a catastrophe occurred.

Gas rationing for cars was in effect because of the war, but since we had a government contract, we could obtain all the aviation fuel we needed. We seldom drove our car, so the gas rationing did not affect us. Our home and airport were located on a rural road which led down McElmo Canyon where there were many fruit orchards. One day one of the ranchers was just about to run out of gas in his car as he was passing the airport. He stopped and asked if I would sell him some aviation gas. I wouldn't sell it, but gave him enough so he could get into town, warning him of the extra high octane of the aviation fuel. He drove off, and I could hear his car going "Pop, Pop, Pop" up the road because of the high octane, but he made it into a gas station in town. The next day he stopped by with a large box of delicious peaches for me and continued to do so every year when his crop was ripe, right up until the time we sold our home.

The Ute Indians had a very low tolerance for alcohol, and liquor was not permitted on the Indian reservation, but they often found ways to get it. When a native drove into our place one day, it was quite obvious that he had been drinking. When I walked out to his car, he told me he needed some gasoline. In a stern voice I said, "Mister, you should not be driving a car." He replied, "Lady, I have to drive, I'm too drunk to walk." Needless to say, he did not get any aviation gas.

We made a lot of charter trips in our planes because of the gas shortage. We would check our destinations with each other in the mornings. One day Rollin took off early with a passenger for Salt Lake City. Later I was making a trip to Los Angeles. I stopped at St. George, Utah, to refuel, and as I was going in for a landing, I noticed Rollin's plane on the ground. He was as surprised to see me as I was to see him. We had lunch together and after a hug and kiss, we each went our separate ways. Today, at eighty-nine, I still smile over how our life together just clicked so beautifully.

FLYING SERVICE ADVENTURES

On one of my scheduled trips, I was to take an elderly man from Cortez to Denver. This would be his first trip in an airplane. I was flying over the high mountains of Cumbres Pass when a gasket in the engine stuck. There happened to be a small town below, but all I could do was to try for a landing on the road, which after some very careful flying, I accomplished. When I looked at my passenger after landing, his face was white as a sheet, but as soon as a crowd gathered, he was telling them about the experience and could hardly wait to get home to tell his grandchildren. In looking around I realized that the road I had landed on was where six years ago, Rollin and I had decided to detour and go to Sante Fe, New Mexico, to be married!

Rollin was on a charter trip to Albuquerque, New Mexico, that morning. I phoned him and he got in touch with an airplane mechanic in Farmington, New Mexico, who was also a flight instructor and owner of the flight school there. The mechanic repaired my plane, and then there was some discussion as to who would make the difficult takeoff from the road and fly the plane back to Cortez. I informed everyone that since it was my plane, it would be my responsibility. They agreed since I was the lightest in weight and I would be most likely to get the plane off the ground in such a short distance. I got behind the controls while the men were on the outside holding tightly onto the wings until I could apply full throttle. Then they released the wings, and I maneuvered the plane very carefully on the narrow road until I felt enough lift to leave the ground and fly gratefully back to Cortez, leaving Rollin to fly my happy, elderly passenger into Denver.

Due to some lack of communication, the mechanic thought I would be landing at his airport in Farmington so that he could check the airplane thoroughly before I continued on to Cortez. When he worriedly called my home a few hours later, I was happily soaking in a tub of hot water, somewhat weary after my day's work.

A forest fire in Ft. Collins near the Denver area brought a request to transport two of the forest rangers from Cortez to Ft. Collins to assist in extinguishing the blaze. Rollin and I took off, each one of us having a fire fighter as a passenger.

It was a hot summer day, and there was a lot of turbulence in the air. I had gone only a short distance when my passenger became airsick. I handed him a container for vomiting (a item we kept in the plane), but whenever my passenger used it, he leaned forward. Since there were flight controls on both sides, while he was being ill, he was also pushing against the controls, forcing the plane to go into a dive. At the same time, I was pulling back on my control to keep the aircraft in level flight or in a climbing mode to gain enough altitude to get over the mountains. Because of the head winds, I had to land in Pueblo to refuel. Going in for a landing upset my passenger's stomach even more. It took all the strength I had to keep the plane in the proper position for landing. After refueling, the attendants at the airport were concerned about my take-off because of the strong wind and suggested they hold on to the wings of the plane until I could apply full throttle and get airborne quickly. I felt sorry for the fire fighter as he looked so ill, but he wanted to continue.

Rollin and I landed at the Ft. Collins airport at approximately the same time. Both of our passengers got out of the plane, went over to the hangar and laid down on the ground. I don't think they were able to fight a fire that day and maybe not even that week. They told us that they would return home on the bus.

Because it had been such a hectic day, Rollin suggested we fly into Denver and spend the night at the Brown Palace Hotel. As I flew over the airport after takeoff, I could still see the two men lying on the ground. After a pleasant evening at the hotel in Denver, we awakened refreshed. The weather the next day was more acceptable, and we had a good flight back home.

Our airport was a very busy place with all the activities, but we decided to have a victory garden as many patriots were doing. On one corner of the airport property, not far from the runway, we planted corn, potatoes, tomatoes, and any vegetables we could think of. We even purchased a cow from a farmer so all interested could have milk. I was even taught how to milk the cow, but I did not do it very often. Since the only food available for the cow were weeds growing around the airport, the milk had a rather weedy flavor.

One day while doing some plowing, Rollin hit a bump and fell from the tractor, breaking his leg. A write-up the next day said:

> When a man bites a dog, that's news, and when a pilot falls off a tractor and breaks a leg, that's news too. R.N. Usher, local banker and pilot with hundreds of safe mountain flying time behind him, is the man who makes such news. He fell from his tractor at the local airport late Sunday evening and fractured his leg.

It did not slow him down much, however, as he could still fly and walk with crutches until he totally recovered.

Our Civil Pilot Training Program was going along very nicely, and we were all pleased. The participants were completing their basic requirements and progressing on into the Air Force. Later we heard that one of them was flying overseas and, although shot down by the enemy, managed to land safely. He, however, was kept in a German prison for some time, and when he finally returned home, he would not talk about the experience.

Two of my women students joined the Jackie Cochran's Womens' Air Service and piloted bombers from the United States to England. I was indeed so proud of those former students of mine.

As a flight examiner it was my policy to know, assuredly, that the pilot could handle a plane in any emergency before issuing a license. One student, who I knew well, had a ranch and a small landing strip near town. He took his flight test with me. I didn't think that he was quite qualified and suggested that he take a few more flying lessons. He was angry and flew over to Grand Junction, and the flight examiner there passed him for a pilot's license. A few months later, I heard that he was flying his family to a Flying Farmer's Convention in the Midwest when he tried to land his plane at the airport located there in rather bad weather. The plane crashed, and he and his family all lost their lives. It was a big loss to our community. It did, however, reinforce my decision that one can never be too careful when it comes to learning how to fly where lives are concerned.

It seemed that everyone around the airport knew how protective I was of my airplanes. One day a young man who was using one of my planes to practice stalled the airplane too close to the ground and crashed into a field near the airport. He had to be taken to the hospital, and when I heard of it, I rushed to the hospital to see how badly he was injured. He was so surprised at my concern, as he thought I would be more upset because he had damaged the plane. It occurred to me that perhaps my concern for people did not show as much as my love for planes, but I was concerned.

A prominent physician in our area took flying lessons and was a good student. When he had the required solo hours for his license, I gave him his final flight test which he passed easily. Even to this day when I am in Colorado and we happen to be in the same group together, he will laughingly tell that when I gave him his flight test, I made him spin the airplane one and a half turns to the left and then one and a half spins to the right, and we did not have parachutes on. The flying service did not have two parachutes at the field as required, but I gave most of the flight examinations in a sixty-five-horsepower plane. The doors on them were not very wide, and it would be difficult to get out of them with a parachute on unless you were quite a small person. So mostly, we didn't bother using them, and never was there a time they were needed.

Our instructor, Frank Brgoch, had a student named Glenn Gregory. He had soloed and was out flying by himself one day when he decided to practice making a forced landing as Frank had taught him. But Glenn made the mistake of letting the plane get too low and flew into some power lines. I was at the field when he returned with wires hanging all over the plane. It was suggested that he go up to our home and explain the situation to Rollin, who was there. Fortunately the plane was not damaged, and Rollin, in a quiet manner, told him that students don't practice forced landings unless they have a flight instructor with them. Later, Glenn went in the service and upon completion, moved to Alaska where he became a bush pilot and an author. A friend in Cortez read one of his books, which related the forced landing incident and mentioned that I had later given him his flight test and license. I was able to contact him in Fairbanks, Alaska, and we have corresponded with each other for more than two years. It was from his encouragement that I decided to write about some of my own flying experiences. The following letter was received from my bush pilot—Glenn R. Gregory—when he heard I was writing my memoirs:

Although I did not fly during WWII, I was fortunate enough to acquire my private license from the school at which Polly and Rollin Usher trained many young men who went on to become WWII Aviators. The school was operating at a much slower pace by the time I entered, which allowed them to spend more time with me to receive the same training. Polly gave me my check-ride and approval for my private license. After returning to Alaska

The Polly Usher Story

I completed my Commercial and Instrument training and flew over 20,000 — all in Alaska. I was well trained and I never caused a passenger to even wear a Band-Aid. I was privileged to receive excellent training from day one with Polly Usher. Not only did I gain much knowledge as a result of her experience, but I had the opportunity to witness a lifetime of incidents such as the time a military U-2, complete with a Chinese pilot had landed, sitting at their airport! I was always impressed by her smooth and confident manner as she operated her airplanes. In my opinion there are few people who have the privilege of having a very pretty, competent lady give a check-ride for a private license, then go on to fly commercially for forty years, and still maintain a very lively and gratifying correspondence with a great lady—Polly.

FASCINATED BY NEW ENGLAND

"Flying Couple" on Brief Vacation Here

New England is by far the most fascinating section of the United States from the air, in the eyes of Mr. and Mrs. Rollin Usher of Cortez, Col., who set down their Taylorcraft plane a few days ago at the North Grafton Airport, to spend a brief vacation with Mr. and Mrs. Lorance P. Salmonsen of 7 Victoria avenue, and Mr. and Mrs. Christian T. Salmonsen of 120 Forest street.

The profusion of lakes, rivulets and vegetation which offers a constant variety of scenic beauties to New England fliers, has spoiled the young aviator and his wife, whose native state is only sparsely endowed with scenic features, in their opinion. Their admiration, however, is daunted by the fact that Worcester as one of New England's representative cities and industrial centers does not own and operate an airport comparable to its status as a municipal center and important geographical position.

"We think the city of Worcester goes on record as being the biggest city with the poorest airport in the country," Mr. Usher stated. "We have landed on fields in little towns with not more than a population of two thousand, which would shame your fair city. Yes, I believe without reservation, that Worcester has the poorest landing field in the country for a city its size," the flier asserted.

Mr. Usher and his wife speak with authority, since both have their private pilot's licenses and have many hours to their credit. Mrs. Usher has done fifty hours of solo flying, and her husband, over one hundred hours. Out West, they are constantly warned of the treacherous Rocky Mountains as flying dangers. As they approached the Eastern seaboard, they were amused to hear warning signals regarding the altitude of the Alleghenies, which, in their hardened lives as high mountain fliers, is hardly worth mention.

Westerners are perhaps more airminded on the whole than Easterners. "In a town like Cortez, for instance, where the nearest railroad is 120 miles away, people take up flying for obvious reasons," Mrs. Usher explained. Her husband is a cashier in the Cortez bank. They are not disheartened, however, by the "God-forsaken" aspects of their home town.

"Why, Hitler couldn't locate us if he tried," Mr. Usher stated amusingly. "We are not war-conscious out there. We just don't worry about it. I can understand why people in the East should be concerned because of the close proximity to the Atlantic. You are in a vulnerable spot," the Westerner contended.

The flying visitors are scheduled to leave today via the North Grafton Airport. They expect to arrive in Cortez, 2600 miles way, within two days, if good weather conditions prevail.

Car and Plane Damaged In Collision at Airport

R. N. Usher, local banker and flying enthusiast, met up with a bit of hard luck Tuesday evening on the local airport when he taxied the Ryan plane, property of Mesa Verde Airways, into his own automobile, doing considerable damage to both plane and car. The plane damage consisted of a broken prop and engine shake-up. The car was badly cut up on the driver's side.

Mr. Usher states that the accident occurred through his being unable to see the parked car from the cockpit. He states that a new motor has been ordered for the Ryan and it will be back in service very soon, in better shape than ever. Bozmans are repairing the damaged car.

TOWN OF CORTEZ AIR-MINDED

What started as a hobby with Mr. and Mrs. R. N. Usher of Cortez, has grown to a thriving business, and their interest has spurred others until Cortez with a population of 2,200 now has 22 planes on its field—percentage record to compare with any city in the state.

Usher is president of the Cortez bank, but in his spare time he works with his flying wife in making charter air trips and in instructing flight students. During the war the Ushers conducted a civil pilot training class and are now training sudents under the GI program.

The Ushers are responsible for the whole town's air-mindedness. It started in 1941 when they bought their first plane, a two-place Taylorcraft. For a while they were the only persons who flew, but they both obtained instructor ratings and started teaching others. Today there are more than 100 persons at Cortez who are able to fly.

Five of the planes at the field belong to the Ushers; 17 are privately owned. This year, with proceeds from a big bean crop, many farmers are purchasing their own planes and learning to fly. And the

HEARD WILLKIE SPEAK TUESDAY

Mr. and Mrs. R. N. Usher returned last evening from Albuquerque where they attended the meeting addressed by Wendell L. Willkie, Republican candidate for president of the U. S. He spoke at Albuquerque Tuesday night en route to California where he is now conducting his campaign. Mr. and Mrs. Usher enjoyed the speech a great deal and described the crowd as being very enthusiastic.

Air Pictures To Be Feature Of Edition

When the Cortez Sentinel Progress Edition, for which orders are pouring in daily, appears the first part of September, a good deal of the success of the publication can be laid in the lap of R. N. Usher, local banker, and his Taylorcraft plane.

Air view pictures of several of the attractions in Southwestern Colorado were in demand by the Sentinel editors and the problem was soon solved when Usher volunteered to fly over the territory.

The plane took off Tuesday morning with Usher at the controls and the Sentinel staff photographer aboard. Within an hour, the desired territory had been circled and photographed, and the plane landed at the local port, having traveled about 120 miles to bring to the Sentinel readers all that they desire and more too.

Remember when . . .

(From our files of 50 years ago)

To Mrs. Polly Usher, wife of R. N. Usher, cashier of the Citizens State Bank, goes the distinction of being the first woman flying student of western Colorado to make a solo flight, as nearly as a checkup on available records will disclose.

Mrs. Usher earned her "wings" when she took the Cub training ship of the Cortez Air School off the local airport Tuesday morning and after circling about the field for several minutes brought it down to a graceful landing that would have been a credit to an experienced pilot.

Remember when . . .

(From our files of 50 years ago - 1945)

A brand new, 1946 model Piper Cub training ship was flown in from Denver yesterday by R.N. Usher who accepted delivery of the new plane at Denver the fore part of the week. It is the first of the new models to be delivered in southwestern Colorado, he reported this morning, and will be followed soon by a new three place cabin ship that will be used as a demonstrator by his local agency for the Piper line of planes.

Mr. and Mrs. Usher flew into Denver Saturday to get the new plane. The dealers were told to anticipate early full production of passenger planes with which they can begin to fill orders of a number of local prospective purchasers anxiously awaiting deliveries.

Cortez Port Made Designated Field

Field Is Now Only One To Authorize Flights

The Cortez airport was marked Tuesday by Civil Aeronautic inspectors Ralph Lovering and Paul Murray, of Denver, as a designated port, and now becomes the only designated port in the San Juan Basin, the Farmington port having lost its designation through lack of activity. The Cortez port won its recognition due to its location on established airlines and removal from surrounding mountains.

With the designation from the CAA, planes taking off from the field can now fly anywhere within a 25 mile radius, where they were previously restricted to a five mile limit.

Previously, if a pilot wished to take up his plane, it was necessary to gain permission from the port at Farmington. Now with the Cortez port designated permission can be secured here for not only flights within the 25 mile radius but for special flights as well. Permission can likewise be secured from here for permission to fly from other ports of the basin.

Also, it is now possible for any licensed civil aircraft to land on the Cortez field, where they previously were restricted. This is especially helpful, according to R. N. Usher, because Cortez is located directly on the airline route between Albuquerque and Salt Lake, a route that has been used quite extensively lately.

May Be Intermediate Field

Since Cortez is now the officially designated port of the basin, a board of registrars and clearance officers has been set up with Mrs. R. N. Usher, Margaret Jordan and Lee Jekyll as members. This will be the board which will authorize flights from all Basin ports in the future.

According to Mr. Usher, O. C. LeBoutillier, chief aeronautic inspector, accompanied by the district airport engineer, will be in Cortez in the near future to make a survey of the local port, with a view to designating it as an intermediate field on established airlines. Should this occur, it would likely result in a large expenditure of federal funds for improvements; a weather station and radio station could possibly come too with such a designation.

Cortez Port Improved

A crew of volunteer workers was at the port Sunday, clearing runways and making other improvements about the field. A near-by building was moved to the field where it will be used as a club-house. Work was started on a hangar to house the plane that was recently purchased by local flying enthusiasts.

Mrs. Usher Meets Courtesy Patrolman

Because her husband "forgot" the little matter of getting a brake and light certificate for his automobile, Mrs. R. N. Usher made the acquaintance of a Colorado Courtesy Patrolman early this week, on the highway between Canon City and Pueblo.

It was a fine day to travel, she was stepping on the gas, when up pops a patrol car from behind, with siren shrieking. Wondering what great crime she had committed Mrs. Usher immediate slowed "Elizabeth" to a walk, then to a stop. Then out steps the minion of the law—none other than good old Tex High, formerly of Cortez.

Says Tex, "You may be from my old town, but you can't get away with that". Says Mrs. Usher "Wait 'till I get hold of that man of mine." After some such "argument" Mrs. Usher was allowed to proceed to Pueblo—where they sell brake and light certificates.

FLIGHT PARTY

A flying party, made up of Mr. and Mrs. H. L. Bigler, Mr. and Mrs. Dan Milenski, Mrs. N. E. Carpenter and daughter, Grace, enjoyed Saturday and Sunday in the Monument valley and if half the things they tell us are true it could all be summed up, "A good time was had by all." Mr. and Mrs. R. N. Usher and "Flying Oscar," from Farmington, were at the controls of the three planes which took the party down.

This is the story of a newspaper story—a detailed account of the humiliation and long hard work a humble reporter must go through to get the news you may or may not read.

Your reporter stopped in at the drugstore for a bracer, and seeing R. N. Usher and Ed Hunter at the counter for refreshment, sat close by in hopes they would say, "Have one on us, fellow,"—which they didn't.

"Did you hear about the forced landing south of town Sunday evening, Scoop?" asked Hunter.

Your correspondent admitted that he had not, and was greeted with a derisive haw-haw by the pair. "A newspaperman and he hasn't heard about the forced landing," they guffawed; whereupon we defended our professional reputation by pointing out that we had until Wednesday night to learn everything we needed to know this week, anyway.

Then we hied to the nearest telephone and called the airport. Caretaker Mahon replied that the only information he had was secondhand. "See Usher," he advised. "He knows the whole story."

Said Mr. Usher, "All I know is that it was my wife's plane. Hattie Johnson was her passenger, and she'll give you all the facts."

Mrs. Johnson finally encountered, referred us to Mrs. Usher, and Mrs. Usher's telephone wouldn't answer. Back to Mrs. Johnson with a plea for the lowdown on the high-up; and that old saw about the ladies liking to talk is missing a few teeth and is generally pretty dull. Mrs. J.'s answers were in modest monosyllables until she came to the point of praising Mrs. Usher's performance in the emergency—then she really loosened up with praise.

It was not until then that we got the story, and a good one it is.

"Polly had kindly offered to take me for a ride," recounted Mrs. Floyd Johnson, "and Sunday evening we took off from the port. We circled to gain altitude. All of a sudden there was a loud noise, and the motor quit. Mrs. Usher calmly surveyed the terrain below, picked out a smooth, level place in a field below, and circling gently on gravity, made the most beautiful deadstick landing I've ever seen.

"I wasn't scared a bit, and now it's over, I'm glad to have had the experience. Polly was magnificent!"

The crankshaft had broken, it was found later; and the plane will be grounded for a week or so for repairs to the engine.

PRESIDENT OF CHURCH GROUP PRAISES LOCAL WOMAN IN PAPER

Reporting on her visit to Western Slope missions in the current issue of the official publication of the Episcopal Diocese of Colorado, Mrs. Clarence C. Moore, president of the Women's Auxiliary of the diocese, writes that the contacts were a wonderful inspiration.

She praised the capable work of Mrs. Polly Usher, president of St. Barnabas Guild, and added the following:

"An you'll be interested to know that she and her husband own an airplane in which they tour about the United States as most of us tour about the mountains in our cars. I'd not be surprised if she was the only Auxiliary president in the American church who travels about in an airplane."

Western Slope Missions Prove Real Inspiration

"It was your President's privilege and joy," says Mrs. Clarence C. Moore, President of the Women's Auxiliary of the Diocese, "to contact personally most of the Western Slope Missions this Fall, and the devotion and enthusiasm of those groups has been a wonderful inspiration. I wish I could take all of you with me on one of these visits. I should like to introduce you to Polly Usher, the President of the Women's Auxiliary at Cortez. Mrs. Usher is a dainty person, so good to look at—and withal so capable. And you'll be interested to know that she and her husband own an airplane in which they tour about the United States as most of us tour about the mountains in our cars. I'd not be surprised if she was the only Auxiliary President in the American Church who travels about in an airplane.

"Then, there's the small group who form the Auxiliary at Cedaredge. They have no church building, and only an occasional service, yet they sent in a Fall United Thank Offering of $13. Isn't that a fine and inspiring thing?"

(Great Guy!)

Citizens State Bank will be hosting a special grand opening in their new main street facilities here this Saturday.

Grand opening festiviites have been scheduled from 11 a.m. to 3 p.m.

Last spring, Charles M. Searle, president of the bank, announced plans for construction of the new location at Main and Chestnut.

Construction work was done by the Perkins Construction Co. of Farmington and completed early this year. The bank moved to the new site several weeks ago.

The building, utilizing Southwestern architecture, provides 10,000 square feet of operating space with an additional 2,000 square feet allocated for tenants and future expansion.

The new bank facility includes a walk-up window, drive-up units, night depository and off-street parking.

Frederick L. Grove of Cortez was the architect.

Citizens State Bank had been located at West Montezuma Avenue.

The bank was opened here in Cortez June 4, 1937 and was then located at the corner of Main and Market Streets, the building which now houses Basin Industrial Bank.

The bank moved to the Montezuma Avenue location in the fifties.

The Montezuma Valley Journal, in the May 28, 1936 issue, reported, "The Citizens State Bank of Cortez will be a going institution by this time next week. R.N. Usher, cashier of the new bank announced this morning that plans now call for the opening of the bank on Thursday, June 4."

"The long awaited certificate of authority issued by State Bank Commissioner Grant McFerson, arrived Sunday, removing all doubts that Cortez was to have a bank.

"J.W. Bozman was elected president of the board of directors and N.E. Carpenter vice-president, at the meeting of the incorporators and stockholders this week. The board of directors is composed of these two and three other incorporators. P.P. Schifferer, C.S. Warren and W.C. Wark.

"Articles of incorporation filed at the courthouse sh— the new bank has a c— stock of $25,000 in 250 —

with 40 stockholders. It will open in the old Montezuma Valley National Bank quarters vacated this week by receiver J.H. King. Work of redecorating and altering the bank building is practically completed."

Citizens State Bank, according to their last statement of condition, deposits totaled $13,266,788.

Usher, the first cashier at Citizens State Bank, came here from Dolores where he had worked at the old J.J. Harris and Company Bank. He sold his bank interests in the fifties and moved to California to make his home. He now resides in Palm Desert, Calif. with his wife, Polly.

..... *notes*

R.N. USHER
—First Cashier
— *cutie* —

PLANES TO ALBUQUERQUE

Mr. and Mrs. R. N. Usher, accompanied by Mrs. Paula Slavens and Ed Hunter, flew to Albuquerque over the week-end for the required 100-hour check-up on the two planes stationed at the Cortez port. The planes, owned by Ushers and the Cortez Flying Club, piloted by Usher and his wife, left Cortez Saturday morning. Mesdames Usher and Slavens returned Sunday; the two men **Monday.**

Local Flying Service Gets New '46 Piper Cub

The Cortez Flying School stepped out last week with the addition of another training ship to its line of airplanes on the local airport.

As agents for the Piper Cub airplane, the local service now has a 1946 model of that ship, the latest to come off the light-plane assembly lines. It was flown into Cortez last wek by R. N. Usher, and during the week has been cruising about over the town.

The Piper Cub is one of the best in light-plane trainers, and will be used locally as a trainer for the classes in aviation. During the war, the army accepted it for many purposes. It was used in the training programs as a pre-flight trainer and many of the United States pilots first took to the air in the small plane. Overseas, the Piper served well. It was flown by liason pilots in support of heavy artillery. And when there was wounded to be transported from battle fields to back-of-line hospitals, Piper was there as an ambulance plane.

This plane is the first of the line of new Piper planes the Ushers have been able to put on the local field. However, the operators are pleased with reports from the manufacturers. They have been told that full production will be under way soon, and all agents will be able to fill the many orders from prospective customers.

Along with the new Piper, the Ushers announce that they will soon have a three-passenger plane here for their use as a demonstrator.

May 17-1943

Down in the southwestern part of Colorado lies the town of Cortez and in this town there is found a pretty and winsome lass who, with 2200 flying hours, a considerable number of civilian students graduated, and two successful forced landings to her credit, has definitely qualified herself in the field of professional aviation. Colorado aviation can well be proud of Pauline (Polly) Usher and her husband-partner, R. N. Usher, for their efforts in building up both private and commercial aviation in the southwest part of the state.

Polly married Mr. Usher in 1937 and both seriously settled down to learn how to fly. After purchasing their first plane in 1941, the Ushers realized the necessity of having more adequate landing facilities near the town and consequently bought the necessary land for a model Class II airport two miles southwest of Cortez. With 5000 foot runways, unobstructed approaches, and courteous service, the operation has developed a fine reputation—particularly with transient pilots from the west and southwestern part of the U.S.

Polly hadn't been flying too long when she was faced with her first forced landing. While blissfully flying over the town of Cortez with another woman passenger, the crankshaft broke and by skillfully slipping, skidding and using excellent judgment, she put the plane down on the only available spot—a field about 100 yards long. When anxious spectators arrived at the plane, Polly was upholding the vanity of her sex by—you guessed it—casually taking off her hose. "Nylons were hard to get" Polly shyly remarked, "I did not want to snag them."

Polly added to her emergency laurals later when a valve stuck on a charter flight over Cumbres Pass. Her passenger was a grandfather on his first plane ride. "He was a grand fellow" Polly said, "Soon" as he collected his wits after we got down on the side of a hill, he acted as official narrator to the crowd which soon assembled."

What with charter flights, instruction, flight examining, and being a housewife, Polly felt she wasn't busy enough so she and Mr. Usher adopted a baby six months ago. She's busy now.

The Ushers anticipate increased air travel in their section of the country during the coming summer months and cordially invite all pilots to drop in and inspect their operation.

CAA Takes Local Airplanes For Navy Cadets at Junction

Action Dims All Hope of Improvement of Airport

The dream of local air enthusiasts of making Cortez one of the air centers of the western slope has been shattered. While our people argued the whys and wherefors of a good airport and our public officials dillied and dallied, treating the port site as an orphan child, Grand Junction, progressive city to the north, got the ear of the U. S. navy and convinced its officials that at Grand Junction was the place for the western slope air base. As a result, all planes from all the airports over the slope are being confiscated by the Civil Aeronautics and taken there to be used in training navy pilots.

Officials from CAA arrived in Cortez Monday and took over planes belonging to R. N. Usher and one owned by local flying club. In addition they are planning to pick up another owned by Charlie Snyder, Dove Creek, and another, the property of Oscar Thomas, local flight instructor. Within the next few days the same officials will pick up all planes in Durango, then take those at Alamosa.

The planes are being taken to Grand Juunction as fast as they are picked up by the government officials. There they will be used in training pilots for the navy, some 150 students being enrolled.

A review of what happened at Grand Junction and what didn't happen at Cortez is of interest. Late in February plans were laid for abandonment of the flight schools at Grand Junction, Alamosa and Cortez. This plan was first revealed by the Sentinel editor who "got next" to the plan while spending a few days in Denver. He immediately advised Cortez men of what was to be expected. Those interested, sought to avert the loss of the Cortez school but public support was not with them. Monday the sad end of what might have been a real asset to the town came about.

Turning to Grand Junction, this town wouldn't be whipped. When the word went out it was to lose its school its chamber of commerce immediately swung into action. A committee was sent to San Francisco to confer with navy chiefs. The city council made an appropriation of several thousand dollars to extend and improve its airport. The town "kept the heat on" and that she finally triumphed is now a matter of record. She will now enjoy the patronage of the students, plus a large personnel of officers and instructors. The school will leave thousands of dollars in Grand Junction.

Cortez airport—if such it may be called—is of no further use, at least for duration. Civilian flyers are grounded because they have no planes to fly; thought of ever getting an army or navy instruction school is, of course, silly to think about in that we do not have even one plane left as a nucleus of equipment. In other words the town has suffered an irrepairable loss, that regrets cannot atone for.

Grand Junction is to be congratulated on getting back her school. She wanted it, she went after it—she got it.

ROMAN WARREN, "The Cowboy Aviator," FLEW A WORLD WAR I PLANE THROUGH A BRIDGE ARCH WITH LESS THAN 36 INCHES CLEARANCE ABOVE AND BELOW! Riverside, Calif., 1926...

Local Pilot in Forced Landing Cumbres Pass

Mrs. R. N. Usher proved her skill as a plane pilot when she set her Taylorcraft plane down Friday on Cumbres Pass in a forced landing. Almost ready to clear the "hump" the plane developed engine trouble. Sighting a small field below Mrs. Usher brought the tiny ship down without damage to it, a passenger, or herself.

Getting in touch with Mr. Usher, who was at Albuquerque at the time, he picked up Oscar Thomas at Farmington and together they flew to the scene of the trouble. The motor was removed from the plane and shipped back to Cortez for repairs. Usher took the passenger on to Denver the next day, bringing in Mrs. Arlene Lien, of Sidney, Montana, who has accepted a position as stenographer in the Milenski & Armstrong law office.

It was fortunate for Mrs. Usher that in making the forced landing, a farm house was nearby, making it possible for her to walk to a telephone with but little effort. The fact that she handled her machine so skillfully is not surprising to acquaintances for she is regarded as one of the best pilots in this part of the state.

Statewide Storms Halt Return Flight Of Cortez People

Still grounded at Alamosa was the report from Mrs. R. N. Usher, pilot of the Cortez plane that has been grounded practically all week because of adverse weather conditions between here and Denver. Her passenger, Ed Hunter, Cortez garageman, is also detained.

They flew to Denver a week ago Wednesday, expecting to return as soon as Mr. Hunter consulted his draft board to see about taking his pre-induction physical examination at this time. By Sunday, however, the storm signals were all against their leaving Denver and they did not get away from that city until Tuesday. When storms blocked their way over the continental divide they returned to the Alamosa airport after several attempts to make the crossing, and there they remain while the San Juan Basin is gripped by another big storm torday.

DURANGO AIRPORT HAS 2 NEW PLANES

MRS. PAULINE USHER, FLYING INSTRUCTOR, TO BEGIN CLASSES

Durango airport now has two new planes in which members of the Durango Flying Club and the Durango Flying Service are taking much pride and pleasure.

One plane, a Taylor Craft ship, has been here about a week, it was flown in from Los Angeles by Harry Fink for the Durango Flying Service.

The other plane, a Funk-Lycoming craft, was flown in Saturday noon from Coffeyville, Kansas, by Hoyte Fuller, for the Durango Flying Club.

Sunday R. L. Beers flew the latter plane to Cortez, where he picked up Mrs. Pauline Usher, who returned with him to Durango. Mrs. Usher will begin a class of instruction in flying at the local airport this week. Already many interested students of flying have enrolled under her.

Ushers Purchase Second Plane to Be Used Locally

R. N. Usher, Cortez' No. 1 flying enthusiast, has returned from California where he purchased two airplanes, one a four-place Waco, the other a two-place Luscombe. The first plane was flown here from southern California by Oscar Thomas, the latter by Mr. and Mrs. Usher.

Both planes are now hangared at the local airport and are being flown every day and evening, much to the enjoyment of the townspeople, those who ride and those who just crane their necks and look.

Mr. and Mrs. Usher, pioneers in the local flying field, recently had their planes taken from them by the C. A. A. when the machines were needed for training naval cadets. They have purchased the new ones in the hope they will be able to retain them. Foreseeing a brilliant future for aviation, the Ushers would like to see a modern port built at Cortez, to put this town on the map, as a progressive western city.

Planes Drop Food to 10 Marooned On Rail-Bus in Colorado Rockies

TELLURIDE, Colo., March 15.—(AP)—Towering snowdrifts closing in around them left 10 persons marooned tonight on a winding narrow-gauge railroad in Southwestern Colorado's storm-swept Rockies. The spot is midway between Montrose and Durango.

THE GALLOPING GOOSE—This is the gasoline-motor-driven rail bus marooned with its driver and passengers on the high narrow-gauge of the Rio Grande Southern Railroad between Durango and Montrose. This is a summer picture of the Goose. Now it's piled high with snow in the southwestern mountains.

Six of the persons had been isolated since Monday afternoon, but fears for the safety of all lessened after two small airplanes today dropped several days' food and medical supplies which the snowbound folk retrieved from the hummocks on 10,200-foot Lizard Head Pass.

Fred Johnson, the Penney store manager at Montrose, his wife and their three-year-old grandson left Dolores Monday for Telluride in the Rio Grande Southern Railway's Galloping Goose with Jimmy Cooper of Ridgway as driver of the automobile converted into a rail car.

Engine Clears Way

Snowdrifts had piled to a height of 15 feet, so railroad officials sent a locomotive ahead of the Goose to clear the tracks. Fifteen miles north of Rico the engine and rail car stalled. Deep snow cut off a return.

Aboard the locomotive were Walter Virden of Rico, engineer, and Mike Smith of Ridgway, fireman.

A second locomotive left Rico yesterday to effect a rescue, but it, too, became marooned. Its four occupants were Engineer W. G. Laube, Fireman Steve Connors, C. R. Rhoades, a Rio Grande Southern foreman, all of Durango, and Alex Vigil of Dolores, a section foreman.

These four were reported to have reached the six other persons on snowshoes. All were understood to have sufficient fuel to keep warm despite near-zero temperatures and high winds. They were without food until today, however.

Mercy Pilots

The mercy plane flights were made by Rollin N. Usher and Joe Piccone, both Civil Air Patrol pilots from Cortez. They dropped six packages. The Johnsons' grandson was understood to require medicine. The pilots said men reached the parcels and dragged them to the snowbound bus.

Additional slides today on the narrow-gauge railroad, which runs from Durango to Ridgway, made it impossible to determine when the 10 persons would be rescued.

A caterpillar roared out of Rico, south of Lizard Head Pass, today with a crew of seven or eight men, while another attempt to cut through to the Galloping Goose was being made from the north by a railroad rotary snowplow from Vance Junction, near Telluride and 11 miles from the pass.

Uses Portable Phone

Attached to the Goose is a trailer in which mail and baggage was hauled. The trailer contains a stove, to keep any perishables from freezing.

In Denver, Cass M. Herrington, receiver for the Rio Grande Southern, reported Cooper, the Goose driver, had communicated with various officials by using a portable telephone device.

Yesterday a State Highway Department crew bucked to within a relatively short distance of the Goose. Herrington said Cooper refused to venture with his passengers from their comparative safety.

DAN HUNTER COVERS "GALLOPING GOOSE"

Dan Hunter, Dove Creek editor, is widely known for his unique manner of writing. The following story relative to recent blockade of the "Galloping Goose" is typical of the literary gems that come from his editorial quill:

"The fiercest snow storm of the centuries swept across the Lizard Head Pass marooning Mr. and Mrs. Fred Johnson and three year old grandson. The Johnsons live at Montrose, the grandson hails from Wyoming.

"The bus, which is called the "galloping goose", pulled out of Rico early Monday morning. The goose was being towed by a D. and R. G. Southern Engine which stalled about four miles West of Lizard Head snowsheds. The engineer, fireman, and the goose herder, realizing the dangerous and precarious condition used portable telephone to hello Rico for food supplies and other relief. Men mounted snow shoes and slowly threaded their windings up the snow covered Pass, knowing that a crack of a whip might loosen an avalanche of snow and ice that would bury them beneath a thousand tons of mountain debris. Nothing daunted these bold mountaineers and at about 9 p. m. Monday the weary laden mountain climbers deposited food at the feet of the famishing "galloping goose," My, what a spread and such a feast!

"Wednesday morning report came that the rotary snow plow had not reached the marooned parties, Banker Usher of Cortez, and Milton Morgan, nozed the Usher plane toward the stars, in their dangerous mercy flight to bring further relief to those who were asunder upon a drift of snow and ice.

" Ed Hunter and Joe Piccone, flying Aces of Cortez, flew within the wake of the Usher plane, as each phantom ship circled the snow-capped summit of old Lizzard Head, dropping their heavenly manna into the lap of the "galloping goose," ere it sang its dying swan song.

"The monster Leviathan of the mountains, the rotary snow plow is supposed to open the road today, Wednesday. Should it fail to reach the unfortunate maroons who have fire in abundance our surmise is that the Cortez Armada of the skies, will once again hover above the 'galloping goose" with its broken wing and frozen toe!"

'The Sky is NOT the Limit'

POLLY USHER is shown here with one of the planes used for instructing students during the early days when Cortez "first got wings" and struggled to obtain commercial air service. She will present a program on her experiences in that era on Sunday evening, June 21, at Mary Blake Hall. An open house will begin at 6:30 p.m., with the program to follow at 7:30. The public is welcome.

Local aviation pioneer to speak Sunday night

Did you know that Cortez' first airport was a small landing field on the east end of Main Street about where the Frontier Motel (now EconoLodge) and Bel Rah (now Budget Host) are located?

A former resident of Cortez, Polly Usher, will recount the early aviation history of our area in a special program entitled, "The Sky is NOT the Limit." She will be here on June 21 and will be presenting her program that evening at Mary Blake Hall at 7:30 p.m. To accommodate her many friends and acquaintances, an open house reception will precede the program at 6:30 p.m., which is also open to the public.

Polly Usher, wife of the late Rollin Usher who put in Citizens State Bank, was one of a minority group of women pilots at that time. She was not only an instructor, but along with other women pilots, ferried planes during the war years to free male pilots for combat duties.

Rollin Usher was also a pilot and aviation enthusiast, and the two were very instrumental in getting an approved airport for the community. This paved the way for Cortez' first commercial air service, Monarch Airlines, later to become Frontier Airlines using the dependable old DC3. She and her husband took their instruction in 1937 from Red Darnall, the man some recall as having one plane and a flying service that mostly operated sightseeing trips around the area. In 1940, Polly began instructing, and some of her "trainees," like Dr. E.C.

See AVIATION on Page 12A

Aviation Continued from Page 1A

Merritt, can recall some exciting moments from that period.

The Ushers were also instrumental in the effort to get lighted runways, essential for commercial service, at the airport, and it was those runway lights that guided a disabled U-2 spy plane to a safe landing in 1959.

Polly Usher came to Cortez with her father, who was the contractor for the building of the first part of the courthouse. Additions to the courthouse were built in later years. Citizens State Bank was started by Mr. Usher in 1936 in the Basin Bank building and later moved to the location on West Montezuma where Valley National Bank is now. Both Rollin and Polly were great enthusiast and promoters of the community and this area.

The public is welcome to attend and enjoy Polly Usher's collage of memories and history of Cortez' early efforts to gain viable air service. Open house on Sunday evening, June 21, at Mary Blake Hall will be at 6:30p.m., with the program to follow at 7:30 p.m.

Flying "Polly" Usher Featured In June Colorado Air News

Mrs. R. N. Usher of Cortez—better known to friends and flying companions as "Polly"—is the subject of a feature article in the June issue of Colorado Air News, state department of aeronautics publication.

Mrs. Usher who, with her husband, son of Mr. and Mrs. N. R. Usher of Florence, operates Cortez Flying Service at Ute Field, has 2,200 flying hours in her piolt's log book and was selected by Colorado Air News as the subject of their June feature because "Colorado can well be proud of her and her husband-partner.

Through the courtesy of Colorado Air News the article is reprinted herewith:

"Down in the southwestern part of Colorado lies the town of Cortez and in this town there is found a pretty and winsome lass.

With 2,200 flying hours, a considerable number of civilian students graduated and two successful forced landings to her credit, she has definitely qualified herself in the field of professional aviation.

Colorado aviation can well be proud of Pauline (Polly) Usher and her husband-partner, R. N. Usher, for their efforts in building up both private and commercial aviation in the southwest part of the state.

After purchasing their first plane in 1941, the Ushers realized the necessity of having more adequate landing facilities near the town and consequently bought the necessary land for a model Class II airport two miles southwest of Cortez.

With 5,000 foot runways, unobstructed approaches, and courteous service, the operation has developed a fine reputation—particularly with transient pilots from the west and southwestern part of the U. S.

Polly hadn't been flying too long when she was faced with her first forced landing. While blissfully flying over the town of Cortez with another woman passenger, the crankshaft broke and by skilfully slipping, skidding and using excellent judgment, she put the plane down on the only available spot—a field about 100 yards long.

When anxious spectators arrived at the plane, Polly was upholding the vanity of her sex by—you guessed it—casually taking off her hose. "Nylons were hard to get," Polly shyly remarked. "I did not want to snag them."

Polly added to her emergency laurels later when a valve stuck on a charter flight over Cumbres Pass. Her passenger was a grandfather on his first plane ride. "He was a grand fellow," Polly said. "Soon as he collected his wits after we got down on the side of a hill, he acted as official narrator to the crowd which soon assembled."

What with charter flights, instruction, flight examining and being a housewife, Polly felt she wasn't busy enough so she and Usher adopted a baby six months ago. She's busy now."—Durango Herald.

Ushers Adopt Child; Arrives Here Saturday To Make Future Home

Mr. and Mrs. R. N. Usher, Cortez, flew to Oklahoma City Friday, returning here Saturday with a 17-day-old girl who they have adopted and taken into their home. Accompanying the Ushers on the flight was Margaret Baze, Cortez.

The child, born in Oklahoma City December 15, has been named Wendy Leigh.

Arrangements for the adoption were made by Dr. Lynn Harrison, Cortez, and now practicing in Oklahoma City.

We have a 'what,' now we need a 'who' on airline

Nate and Norma Wilcox of Mancos recently brought a solution to at least one part of a mystery photograph published earlier this year in the Cortez Newspapers.

The photo shows an old plane with "Mesa Verde Airways Cortez, Colo." on it. It was believed that regular airline service was fur- nished here during or before World War II.

The Wilcoxes recently received a letter from their friends, Wayne and Dee Melgreen of Tucson, Ariz.:

"Dear Nate and Norma,

"Received your letter of 6-21-87. The aircraft pictured is evidently a Ryan B-1 'Brougham.' The B-1 was a successor to the Ryan M-1 and M-1 and in the development stage when Lindbergh ordered the NYP (Spirit of St. Louis).

"Work was stopped on the B-1 to produce the NYP, whereupon com- pletion of the Lindbergh order, work resumed on the B-1 and it went into production. This was circa 1926-27.

"The fuselage, tail surfaces and landing gear of the D-1 design were incorporated into the 'Spirit of St. Louis.' The picture of your plane shows modifications and changes from the original B-1, such as a tail wheel instead of tail skid, removal of wide fairings and cuffs from lift struts and landing gear assembly (possibly a wider fore-and-aft L.G. vee strut assembly) and of course you have air wheels instead of the faired high pressure tires of that era. The original engine was and ap- pears to be a J-5 Wright.

We put your letter on the bulletin board and it was first correctly iden- tified by David Killough of Texas who has a Cardinal at our place and is old enough to remember such things. Further verification from Aviation Quarterly, Vol. 3, No. 3."

An important question - what - has been answered on the plane.

Still unanswered are who, when, where, why and how.

Any answers will be appreciated by the Cortez Newspapers, Inc.

Can you remember this airplane? . . .

PARKED at a local field, this "Mesa Verde Airlines" plane marked as being headquartered in Cortez is in an unidentified photo owned by the Cortez Newspaper. A reader in the accompanying letter iden- tified what type of plane it is, but being sought in addition is more information about the date and the operations and owners.

BY BYRON McKELVIE

"Mesa Verde Airways," probably the Cortez area's first "airline," has been identified.

A photograph of an airplane bearing the words "Mesa Verde Airways, Cortez, Colo.," was sent to the Cortez Newspapers earlier this year. However, no one seemed able to remember such a service being here.

Recently, Mrs. Polly Usher explained that she and her late husband, R.N. Usher, along with Red Darnell had bought the airplane in the 1930's, using it for charter flights for a time.

She recalled that the late J.W. Ertel and his wife, Edna, were on a flight with Darnell to Denver one time when the plane went down due to technical failure. They were reported lost and then found. Finally the Ushers and Darnell sold the plane.

R.N. Usher, who helped organize and start the Citizens State Bank in 1936, was an avid supporter of flying and helped develop aviation in Cortez.

Mrs. Usher, who learned to fly, served as an instructor at the Cortez Flying Service for many years. She now lives in Palm Desert, Calif., but spends the summers in Cortez.

Lindbergh-type plane in Cortez. . .

MESA VERDE AIRLINES' "fleet" was this Ryan B-1 Brougham, a sister ship of the famous Lindbergh "Spirit of St. Louis." The plane was used for charter flights in the 1930's from the Cortez airport located east of town about where the Rauh Motel now stands.

Cortez aired plans for airline back in 1930's

BY BYRON McKELVIE

"Mesa Verde Airways," probably the Cortez area's first "airline," has been identified.

A photograph of an airplane bearing the words "Mesa Verde Airways, Cortez, Colo.," was sent to the Cortez Newspapers earlier this year. However, no one seemed able to remember such a service being here.

Recently, Mrs. Polly Usher explained that she and her late husband, R.N. Usher, along with Red Darnell had bought the airplane in the 1930's, using it for charter flights for a time.

She recalled that the late J.W. Ertel and his wife, Edna, were on a flight with Darnell to Denver one time when the plane went down due to technical failure. They were reported lost and then found. Finally the Ushers and Darnell sold the plane.

R.N. Usher, who helped organize and start the Citizens State Bank in 1936, was an avid supporter of flying and helped develop aviation in Cortez.

Mrs. Usher, who learned to fly, served as an instructor at the Cortez Flying Service for many years. She now lives in Palm Desert, Calif., but spends the summers in Cortez.

Red Darnell, another old-time pilot, died in California several years ago.

Recently, Nafa and Norma Wilcox of Mancos received a letter from Wayne and Dee Melgreen of Tucson who identified the airplane as a Ryan B-1 Brougham, which was sort of a sister ship of Charles Lindbergh's famous "Spirit of St. Louis," which was built in the mid 1930's.

Cortez residents evidently continued to try to get airline service.

A 1944 Cortez newspaper reported that Mountain States Aviation, Inc., of Denver got its Colorado Public Utilities Commission permit to provide daily flights here starting by Sept. 1.

Mountain States proposed a flight linking Denver, Leadville, Glenwood Springs, Grand Junction, Cortez, Durango, Alamosa and Canon City.

"It will be noted," the article said, "in the following from the Denver Post that Cortez is far ahead of some towns in the matter of having an airport site and certain improvements and services that have been maintained during the while other towns were closing existing airports or failing to acquire sites until now."

The article also reported that the southern route of Mountain States Aviation would duplicate part of the service of the recently approved airline of S.N. Drum of Durango.

Apparently, Mountain States Aviation's plan to serve Cortez never got off the ground, so to speak. However, starting in 1949, Cortez had a love affair for 32 years with Frontier Airlines, which started out as Monarch Airlines.

It began to sour in 1959, when Frontier appealed to the Civil Aeronautics Board to withdraw service to Cortez. A small Westair took over for a few months until it no longer could economically operate the route, and Frontier took over Cortez flights again.

Deregulation in 1978 put the squeeze on Frontier Airlines. Frontier pulled out of Cortez for good in 1982.

But there had been previous attempts at establishing another airline's service in addition to Frontier's.

For instance, in the mid-1960's, the Cortez newspaper announced that Navajo Airline started a route from Las Vegas, Nev., to Grand Junction with stops at Cortez, Monticello, Nucla and Moab.

It was the first time that a commercial airliner had ever landed at Monticello, Moab and Nucla.

Scheduled to make the initial flight were Vic Reynolds, president of the airline; Norman Kessler, operations manager; stockholders Jim Cooper and A.W. Hutchings; Rocky Clarke; Tommy Reynolds; Cal Baxter; and Russ Brown.

Members of the board of directors of the airline included I.L. Gov. Stephen R. McNichols, D.L. Williams, Wayne Denny, Clarence Walizky, A.W. Hutchings, Jim Cooper, T.B. Skidmore and R.N. Usher.

Navajo Airline was short-lived.

With the pullout of Frontier, Pioneer Airlines and Trans-Colorado Airlines took over service to Cortez in 1981. Pioneer later discontinued serving Cortez. Recently, Mesa Airlines came to offer service, but only stayed a short time.

Trans-Colorado, now Continental Express, continues to serve Cortez.

Lindbergh-type plane in Cortez. . .

MESA VERDE AIRLINES' "fleet" was this Ryan B-1 Brougham, a sister ship of the famous Lindbergh "Spirit of St. Louis." The plane was used for charter flights in the 1930's from the Cortez airport located east of town about where the Rauh Motel now stands.

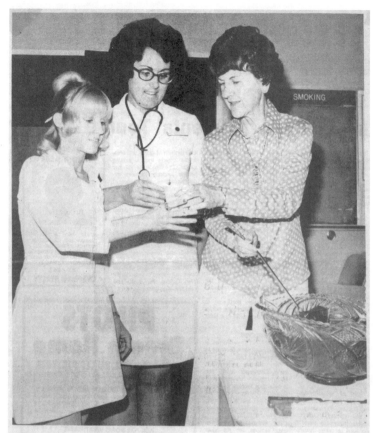

FIRST CLASS — Polly Usher (right) of the Eisenhower Medical Center nursing education department, pours a cup of fruit punch for Linda Everett (left) of Morongo Valley and Mary Beckner, Palm Springs — two of eight graduates of EMC's first class for nursing assistants. An informal reception was held to honor the graduates of the eight-week course covering duties of nursing assistants. Not pictured are Penny Aldridge, and Deborah Foreman of Desert Hot Springs, Mario Garza and John Navarro of Indio, Mary Fulton, Twentynine Palms and Shirley Torres, Banning.

Monument Valley—Navajo Land

Digging Arrowheads

Monument Valley

Polly's Catfish catch

Monument Valley

Camping

Rainbow Bridge

Four Corners

Bankers Convention

FLYING UTES PLAN "FLY-IN" BREAKFAST

About one hundred and fifty people are expected to attend the "Fly in Breakfast" that is to be sponsored by the Flying Utes in Cortez on June 25th.

The Utes will start serving breakfast at 8:00 o'clock. They will judge the spot landings that are made. Each entry is allowed only one chance. There will be prizes for the best landing and a free auto trip to Mesa Verde.

The Flying Utes have invited the famous Flying Farmers and expect many from the eastern slope and a large number from this area.

Rollin's Parents—Edith and Newell

Polly's Parents—Alfred and Elsa Marie

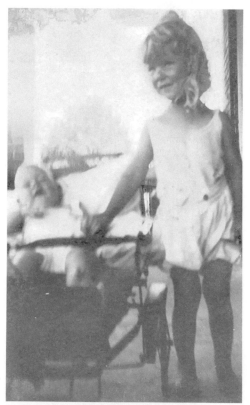

Polly (standing) and baby brother "Irving Ralph"

Polly's Family—From left to right: Michelle, Wendy, Polly, Erika

Polly, we just want to say...

...that your program on your life as an Aviatrix was awe-inspiring and very well-told! It was exciting to learn about the history of Aviation in America through the eyes of a women!

Thanks so very much.

Lovingly in PEO,

Your Sisters from the Coachella Valley Group

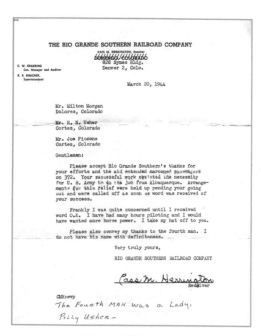

THE RIO GRANDE SOUTHERN RAILROAD COMPANY

CASS M. HERRINGTON, Receiver

~~DURANGO, COLORADO~~
828 Symes Bldg.
Denver 2, Colo.

C. W. GRAEBING
Gen. Manager and Auditor

R. R. BOUCHER,
Superintendent

March 20, 1944

Mr. Milton Morgan
Dolores, Colorado

Mr. R. N. Usher
Cortes, Colorado

Mr. Joe Piccone
Cortez, Colorado

Gentlemen:

Please accept Rio Grande Southern's thanks for
your efforts and the aid extended marooned passengers
on 372. Your successful work obviated the necessity
for U. S. Army to do the job from Albuquerque. Arrangements for this relief were held up pending your going
out and were called off as soon as word was received of
your success.

Frankly I was quite concerned until I received
word O.K. I have had many hours piloting and I would
have wanted more horse power. I take my hat off to you.

Please also convey my thanks to the fourth man. I
do not have his name with definiteness.

Very truly yours,

RIO GRANDE SOUTHERN RAILROAD COMPANY

Cass M. Herrington
Receiver

CMH:evp

The Fourth MAN was a Lady,
Polly Usher —

GROUNDED

In the town of Dolores, which was eleven miles north of Cortez, there was a narrow gauge railroad track and a small train that had been constructed from a Pierce Arrow car. It made scheduled trips from Dolores over the high mountains to Montrose, Colorado. One exceptionally cold winter day the train became stranded on a nine-thousand-foot mountain pass because of a snowstorm. Friends of ours were on the train with their infant grandson. Word came to us that the baby was ill, so we flew up and dropped food and medicine near the engine of the train so the passengers could survive until rescued. I have a letter from the Rio Grande Southern Railroad dated March 20, 1944, commending us for undertaking such a dangerous mission. But these things you are inspired to do when a friend is in need.

In the midst of our Civil Pilot Training, we were shocked when a government representative came to Denver to tell us that they were going to have to shut down some of our schools. They would also be taking our planes for a Navy Cadet program in Grand Junction, Colorado. They said that they would pay us a price, determined by them, and the planes would be taken within two days. We were in complete shock!

The evening before the planes were to be confiscated, a group of us gathered at the airport to commiserate with each other. We decided to take our planes up for the last flight. Rollin and I went up in our Pansy aircraft, and I still, to this day at age eighty-nine, remember the grief I felt. The next morning we watched, helplessly, as the planes were taken away. We were completely grounded! What we thought and knew to be ours, was now gone!

Durango, a town forty miles east of Cortez still had airplanes. I was asked if I would come over there to give lessons. The following is a comment in their local paper:

Durango has two airplanes. Mrs. R. N. Usher of Cortez is presently at Durango where she has a class of students enrolled for flying instructions. Durango had thus far been fortunate in not having their planes requisitioned by the government, so while they are still there, many San Juan Basinites are taking advantage of the chance to add to their hours of flying. Mrs. Usher will begin a class of instruction in flying at the local airport this week. Already many interested students of flying have enrolled. Mrs. Usher is highly qualified as an instructor and the Durango Airport is fortunate to secure her services.

Durango is a most attractive town, located in a mountain valley. The airport at that time was located on a mesa, a few hundred feet above the valley floor. The airstrip was not very long, but because of the elevation of the airport, when one came to the end of the runway, the plane was in the air, and the pilot just had to lower the nose of the plane to build up airspeed and gain altitude. It was an interesting place to give flying lessons. I had both women and men students, and I gave lessons four days a week, staying at the nice Statler Hotel located in town. When I was through, I would drive back home to my handsome husband over the weekend.

Many years later (about 1983) I was spending the summer in Cortez when a good friend John Dickson, who had a plane, invited me to fly with him to Durango to witness an air show. While there, I was surprised to have gray-haired men who had been young students of mine, come up and ask me to autograph their log books. It was fun to see them again.

IN THE AIR AGAIN

We were not happy with having our airport without planes. After all, airports are for airplanes, so we were determined to try to do something about it. Los Angeles was in a complete blackout because of the war, and private planes were grounded. We decided to go there and see if we could purchase some of the unused planes. Staying at the hotel in Los Angeles and looking out the window at night to see nothing but darkness was a strange sight, but we did locate some available planes. We got permission to fly out a two-place Luscombe and a four-place Waco plane, so we were back in business again.

Flying Joyfully

I had many relatives in Denver, sisters, brothers, nephews and nieces, my mother and dad, and Rollin's parents in Florence, Colorado. All enjoyed flying with us. Two of my nephews, Phil and Bill, later became colonels in the Air Force. They and their wives, Sally and Ann, and sister Lynne are now very close friends.

Our most eager passengers were my mother and father. They had relatives living in Bradenton, Florida, and my dad suggested that we all fly there in our Waco plane for a visit. The day before we were to leave, Rollin took the plane up to check it out, and when he landed, the plane ground-looped, turning quickly to the right after it touched the ground. He took the plane up again to test it, with the same result. We decided it was not a plane to fly cross-country with two cherished passengers, so it seemed the trip was off. My father suggested that since we couldn't go by plane, we take the train instead. I had never been on a train before, so it sounded like a new and different sort of adventure. We did have a delightful two weeks, enjoying the excellent food served and sleeping in the bunks. The rumble of the train did not disturb us, and the relatives in Florida were happy to have us visit. We promised, however, that the next time we would bring our plane.

When the Navy Cadet program in Grand Junction was completed, we were notified that we could have our planes back for the same price which the government had paid us. As soon as we received the news we all headed for Grand Junction and flew the eight planes back to Cortez. Of course, I was at the controls of my beloved Pansy aircraft. I was totally elated as I flew her back home. I knew that Pansy and I could not be parted for long as we had been through a lot together. She was mine and I was hers! She seemed none the worse for her experience and our flight school was open for business again.

"Bonanza" A Polly Favorite

EXPANSION

The price of airplanes was not high at that time, ranging from six hundred dollars to six thousand dollars, depending on the plane. Insurance was not required, and because we had our own mechanics, we never carried insurance. Gasoline was inexpensive, and since we always took the shortest route to our destination, the trips were also inexpensive.

By this time we had the planes needed for instruction: two-place Piper Cubs, a Luscombe, one three-place Piper Cruiser. We had also purchased four-place planes for our own pleasure and charter trips. We sold the Waco and bought a very solid Stinson and later a Beechcraft Bonanza, which became our favorite.

Flying Joyfully

We flew back to the Beechcraft Factory to bring it home. It was decided that we would take the airline from Denver to Detroit. It was to be my first trip on a commercial airline. I dressed in my finest dress, which was expected at that time, with hat and gloves. Rollin wore a suit, but not a necktie as he was not a necktie man.

The airline took off carefully and made a slow, easy ascension as they were trying to get people used to flying with them and didn't want to upset them in any way. We were served two delicious meals between Denver and Detroit, and the hostesses were so attentive. All had degrees in nursing at that time. We spent the night at Ford's lovely Dearborn Inn, and the next day, flew our beautiful plane from the factory to our home. She became part of the family. Life was good, and I wrote the following in my log book on my twenty-ninth birthday:

> *This ends another log book and one of the happiest years of my life. I know I shall someday look back with pleasure on the good times and the satisfaction which I have had instructing students. My students number twenty and we have eight planes. It will be interesting to note the growth of aviation in the next twenty-five years.*

NAVAJO FIRE DANCE

Shortly after the war was over and the men who served our country so gallantly were returning home, we had a phone call from the Gouldings inviting us to come to the valley for a special occasion. The Navajo Indians were planning to hold a fire dance in honor of the Navajos who were in the service, and it would probably be the last fire dance that would ever be held.

The Navajo men were very valuable during the war as they could transmit information in there language, and not be understood by the enemy troops. We surely were not about to miss the opportunity to witness the last spectacular fire dance to be performed by the natives, so on the evening of the event, Rollin and I shared the same plane and flew to Monument Valley. When it became dark, we with the Gouldings and a few other guests, got into thier van, and Harry drove us to the location in the desert where the ceremony was to be held. There a tepee had been erected and logs laid out for a fire. Soon after we arrived, the fire was ignited, and when it was in flames, a group of Navajo men, naked except for a loin cloth, their bodies painted white with asbestos pigment, and lovely Indian designs painted on their backs, came running into the fire area from all directions.

They began their native dancing and chanting, circling the fire. Some squaws emerged from the tepee with long branches, which the men ignited from the fire, and continued their dancing, which became more frenzied as time went by. Then they began striking their own bodies and those of the other dancers with the flame torches. As the hours went by, the dancing became more active, and a beautiful sight those who were watching would never forget. We sat in the van, looking out the windows completely mesmerized.

At the first light of dawn, all of the Navajo dancers ran to their horses, which had been tethered nearby, jumped up onto their backs, and rode off shouting into the sunrise.

I thinks our spirits had been a part of the dancing, also, and it was a little while before we could come back to the present and start our drive back to the lodge.

Having been up all night, we were ready for bed and laughing decided that whoever awakened first would have to cook our breakfast. But, as usual, after a long, peaceful sleep, we were awakened by the wonderful fragrance of Mike's breakfast cooking and knew it was time for us also to arise.

The Polly Usher Story

The conversation around the breakfast table was entirely about the magnifiicent Navajo fire dance, and how forunate we were to have been present at such an unforgettable event.

BEYOND AIRPLANES

One day a helicopter stopped at our airport. They were called "whirlybirds" at that time, and of course, we were interested in taking a ride and seeing if we could fly it. Rollin went up first and came back with a big smile on that handsome face. When I got into the whirlybird with the instructor, he told me that my husband tried to take the helicopter off sideways and backwards, and that wasn't the way to do it. Later, I learned how he could have done that, as the aircraft was quite difficult to fly. One had to use both hands and feet at the same time, which was different from the planes we flew where we used the left hand on the wheel and the left foot on the rudder pedal to make a left turn and the opposite for a right turn.

Flying Joyfully

I did manage the proper takeoff on the whirlybird and enjoyed seeing the ground drop beneath us on the ascent, but truthfully, I never had the urge to fly one again. When I asked Rollin about his sideways and backward takeoff he replied, "Well, you know I like to be different."

Also I had an occasion to perform crop dusting at one time, but that too was not in my category of fun. Later, it was said that my first flight instructor, Carl Darnall, died of lung infection caused from inhaling the insecticides used in dusting crops.

In the winter, when the snow was deep, we put skis on the planes and kept flying.

Several years later, when in Albuquerque one day, we had the unique experience of flying a French JAL plane which was a small jet plane. I was surprised at the speed of it and how quickly it executed a turn. It was amazing.

AND BABY MAKES THREE

Our life of doing what we wanted to do, when we wanted to do it, was going to change for the better.

Rollin's assistant cashier at the bank, Pete Dunlap, and his wife were very close friends of ours. They did not have any children either and decided to adopt. A young man, Henry Harrison, who had lived in Cortez and was a Mesa Verde park ranger, later became a physician and moved to Oklahoma City. He notified the Dunlaps that he had delivered a baby girl who was up for adoption. Also, his brother was an attorney in the city and would take care of all the legal matters.

Flying Joyfully

Pete and Buff were very excited, and we offered to fly Buff back to Oklahoma City to pick up the baby while Pete took care of the bank. On October 16, 1947, we took off in our Stinson plane with Buff and Dr. Harrison's sister, who had volunteered her services so that someone with experience in handling a baby would be with us.

Upon reaching Oklahoma City, we went to the hospital and were taken to see an adorable baby with large brown eyes and lots of brown hair. We all fell in love with her at once. Rollin was so impressed that he said to Dr. Harrison, "Hank, why don't you get us one of these?"

He answered, "As a matter of fact, I have one available in December."

We both replied, "We'll take it." It seemed too good to be true that with all the wonderful things in our life that we were now also going to be parents! Buff had named her daughter Carol Lynne, and Pete was at the airport to meet us on our return to greet this beautiful baby girl.

That evening while we were having dinner, Rollin had second thoughts and questioned if we should really adopt a child. His reasoning: "Do you realize that when the child is eighteen years old, I will be sixty-five years old?"

I assured him that he was going to be sixty-five in eighteen years whether we adopted a baby or not.

Then he asked, "Why, with all you have to do, would you want the responsibility of being a mother?"

I said to him, "I don't want to be alone in my old age." That ended the conversation between us.

On December 15, 1947, we received a call from Dr. Harrison informing us that we had a beautiful baby girl. She would have to remain in the hospital for ten days, and since we were scheduled to go to a banking convention in Salt Lake City, Utah, the next day, we went ahead and made the commitment. That evening while we were at the bank party at the Hotel Utah, Rollin mentioned that I was going to have a baby next week, and some of the men didn't know whether they could ask me to dance or not., although I did not appear pregnant.

We flew to Oklahoma City on December 26, 1947, also accompanied by Dr. Harrison's sister. When we got to the hospital, we found that the nurses did not want to part with this lovely, blue-eyed, blonde baby girl. She had been in their care for ten days, and they had named her Fifi and had become very attached to her. Looking at this beautiful, tiny infant, I felt some apprehension and said to Rollin, "I don't know if I am qualified to take care of such a precious baby." He put his arms around me and assured me that if the Indian women on the reservation could raise their young, even in mud huts, that with all of my qualifications, I wouldn't have any trouble being a good mother.

The nurses gave us a bottle of milk for our return trip, and we went back to the airport and took off in our Beechcraft Bonanza. After we were in the air, I tried to feed this new baby but she refused to take the bottle. I guess she was intelligent enough to recognize a novice when she saw one. Our friend Dr. Harrison's sister, who was in the back seat, suggested she take over and proceeded to feed the little infant with no problem. I was so thankful that she was with us and I soon learned to accomplish this needed privilege.

My friend who now lives in Alaska was in the airport office when we got home. He says that he shall never forget the huge smiles on both Rollin's and my face when we walked in with that tiny bundle. He asked to hold her, and I reluctantly handed her to him but kept my hands underneath the blanket at all times. I was so afraid that he might drop her, an indication that I was going to be as protective of our daughter as I was of our airplanes. She was to be, and still IS, the JOY of my life. By the time we reached home, she had already wrapped strings around Rollin's heart. She was Daddy's girl, for sure. Whenever I would get up during the night to feed her, he would get up also. I suggested that maybe we could take turns. He was delighted to have his turn of holding the bottle by himself but still arose to watch me feed her.

An article in *Airplane News* stated:

> What with charter flights, instructing, flight examiner, and being a housewife, Polly Usher wasn't busy enough, so she and Mr. Usher adopted a baby girl six months ago. She is busy now. The Ushers expect increased travel in their section of the country during the coming summer months and cordially invite all pilots to drop in and inspect their operation."

We named our daughter Wendy Leigh. Rollin picked the name Wendy, and a close friend suggested that Lee would go well as a middle name. He agreed but insisted that it be spelled "Leigh."

I would put her bassinet in the back seat of my plane while giving lessons or, if I was making a short charter trip, could leave her with our mechanic's wife, who lived in a house at the airport. She had no children of her own and was devoted to baby Wendy.

Rollin and I had flown to Marble Canyon, Utah, many times. The boat trips down the river ended at Mexican Hat. Harry

Goulding's cousin, Art Greene, and his wife owned the lodge there and had a small airstrip also. We flew there whenever they were putting on a "buffalo roast," and it was one of our favorite trips for our Sunday morning Flying Club. One day, Art suggested to Rollin that he try to get an airplane engine for his boat so trips could be made up the canyon to Rainbow Bridge. This occurred not many months after we had brought Wendy home from Oklahoma City.

Arrangements were made for Joseph Muench, a very well-known photographer, his wife, Joyce, and young son, David; Art Greene and his wife; and Rollin and me to make the first trip up the river to Rainbow Bridge. One part of me said, "You can't just leave Wendy with a baby sitter to go to such an isolated area," and the other part of me, countered, "But you simply cannot miss this trip of a life-time." The young girl who was our baby sitter lived just a short distance down the road from our home, and her mother told me that she would help in the caring of Wendy. So after saying several prayers, Rollin and I took off in our plane for Marble Canyon.

The airplane engine was installed on the rear end of the boat with an Indian name, "Tesh Na Ni Sh Go Afia," which translates to, "Trail to Rainbow Bridge." We departed from Lees Ferry on the first trip to be made through Glen Canyon, up the Colorado River, on 1,360 miles of twisting rapids to reach Rainbow Bridge.

It was a spectacular sight from the very beginning—traveling up the river and looking up at the colorful canyon walls. All of us were entranced with the beauty and there was little conversation among us.

When evening came, we made camp along the shore of the river, built a campfire, cooked and ate a delicious dinner, and then sat around the campfire, talking until we all decided it was time to close out the beautiful day we had been through and climbed into our sleeping bags. We lay there looking up at the thousands of brilliant stars in the black sky,until we drifted into a sound sleep and awakened when the sun rose over the rim of the canyon wall.

We all quickly got out of our sleeping bags, ready to start another day of magnificent beauty. Some willow sticks were found and we put a line and a fish hook on them, caught some fish from the river, which we cooked over the campfire for our breakfast. The fish were delicious.

Having finished our breakfast, we packed up our supplies, got back into the boat, and continued on our journey up the river until we reached the stream that led to Rainbow Bridge. The boat was tied down along the river, and we started the two mile hike to the base of the monument. I had seen Rainbow Bridge many times from the air but still was not prepared for the breath-taking experience of standing below and looking up to its towering height of 309 feet. Rainbow Bridge is a natural wonder of red rock. Its span is 278 feet and the rock 42 feet thick at the top of the arch—an awe-inspiring sight.

When we could finally bring ourselves to leave that treasured ground, we hiked back to the boat to start our return trip to Lees Ferry. There was only one scary incident when Joyce Muench, who was a very active woman, jumped out of the boat at one stop to get closer to the canyon wall for a picture and landed in some quicksand. The sand quickly engulfed her, up to her knee caps, and would soon have covered her whole body had not her husband called to her to lie down and roll, which she did, and managed to free herself from the sand. We continued our trip down to the lodge and Rollin and I flew our plane back home from there. I don't know how many people, if any, were able to make that same trip as, when the

Glen Canyon Dam was built some years later, this area became a lake and all the spectacular canyon walls are now under water.

I thought about Wendy a lot during our trip, of course, but in retrospect, I had such a memorable trip that it will be in my mind forever. I also know that our daughter, now a beautiful, healthy woman, suffered no harm from the short separation from her parents.

THE YOUNG FLYER

When Rollin was flying, his favorite passenger was his beautiful daughter. He started a log book for her, and when she was two years old, she had her picture in the newspaper as having two hundred flight hours to her credit.

I did not want there to be any secrets between us and have her one day, as an adult, discover that she was adopted. So while she was in her high chair and I was feeding her spoonful by spoonful, (and I am sure long before she could really understand what I was talking about), I told her of our wonderful airplane flight to Oklahoma to bring her home as our very own. Also, she and Carol Lynne

103

were inseparable friends through their childhood, and they were both happy with their parents.

Whenever we took a trip, Wendy and Carol Lynne would be in the back seat of our Beechcraft Bonanza. Carol Lynne would often get air sick and vomit on Wendy's favorite stuffed pet that she was taking along on the trip, which caused some problems. But mostly, they had fun playing at the pool in Phoenix or wherever we went for a trip.

Wendy did not like being fastened by a seat belt. We kept a blanket in the back seat of the plane so the girls wouldn't get cold, and she would snuggle up in the blanket and release the seat belt. I was somewhat aware of that, but as long as the belts were fastened on takeoff, I didn't say anything. One day we were flying to Phoenix, and there was a loud thump against the airplane, and something damaged the propeller. I immediately turned toward the back seat and said, "Wendy, fasten your seat belt now!"—which she did. We landed at Phoenix to discover a large eagle plastered against the side of the plane. We were indeed fortunate not to have sustained serious damage to the plane that could have caused even greater problems.

We would fly over the mountains to Florence, Colorado, as often as we could to visit Rollin's parents as they enjoyed Wendy as much as we did, and there was great love among all of us. One wintry day in December, we were making a return flight after spending the weekend with them. We were flying over the mountain pass when our propeller stuck in low pitch. We had some power, but not enough to maintain or gain altitude.

We were not far from the mountain town of Gunnison, Colorado, but the runway was covered with deep snow. We circled the airport a couple of times and those on the ground realized that we were in trouble and needed to land. Soon, we saw a tractor arriving from town to clear the runway for us. Wendy, realizing that something was wrong, started crying in the back seat, so I lifted her up front to sit on my lap and to comfort her. She vomited all over my fur jacket, but that was of no concern at that time.

In the meantime, the tractor made one clearing pass down the runway and Rollin followed directly behind him making a perfect landing just as we used our last drop of gasoline and the engine quit. The airplane had to be towed to the hangar where, luckily, they had a mechanic who was able to repair the plane.

The temperature in Gunnison was forty degrees below zero that night. We checked into a local hotel, and the three of us snuggled together in the same bed, just happy to be safe again. With the airplane repaired, we were able to fly home the next day.

GROWING UP IN THE BACK SEAT
As Told By My Daughter
Wendy Usher Johnson

From as far back as my memory serves, I remember being bundled up before dawn and whisked away to the airport. When I was very small, I was allowed to sleep in the back seat of our car while Mother and Daddy pushed our plane out of the hangar and prepared for their flight to wherever. It seems that we went somewhere every weekend, weather permitting and sometimes weather "not permitting." During the summer we flew to Monument Valley; during the winter, when cabin-fever had got the better of us, we flew to Phoenix. By the time I was two years old, I'd logged over two hundred hours in the air and had my picture in the newspaper, standing all dressed up on the wing of our plane.

Flying Joyfully

I remember "my" first plane. It was a blue and silver Beechcraft Bonanza with the Y-tail. It was eight-four-zero-six-alpha (N8406A). I heard the number repeated so often I'll never forget it. When I was four or five years old, Daddy bought a newer plane, a red and silver Bonanza, and it had little duck-shaped light deflectors on the wing tips, which I thought were soooo cute. (Never mind that it was a better plane.) I don't remember its number.

Sometimes we'd take my best friend along, but she always got airsick and rarely hit the "burp can" (a small white cardboard cylinder similar to an ice cream carton with a smaller opening). Once when we went to Phoenix, she threw up on my favorite stuffed animal, and I refused to get rid of it, so we made the entire trip with the awful smelly thing. When we got home Mother tried to wash it, but by then it was so permeated with the stench, it was unsalvageable. Only then did I finally consent to throwing it out.

Mother always insisted that I wear my seat belt whether or not I was sleeping. In truth, I hardly ever did. As soon as we took off, I'd cover myself up with a blanket and undo the seat belt. The back seat was only about four feet long, and the seat belt was uncomfortable and restrictive. Besides, where could I go but up?

The one and only time I ever remember obeying her was one winter when we flew to Phoenix. At some point just before we got there, Mother turned to me as white as a sheet and said, "Wendy, put your seat belt on TIGHT!" I knew instinctively that something was wrong so I complied. As it turned out, an eagle had flown directly into the nose of the plane and had, in turn, broken the propeller. We literally landed on a "broken eagle wing and a prayer." The entire Phoenix airport crew came running when we landed. Of course, I didn't know anything about the eagle until much later, so I thought we had become celebrities or something!

One of my absolute favorite things was to get Daddy to do the roller coaster. He would fly really high and then descend really fast, and for a few moments—without the seat belt and underneath the cover of the blanket—I'd be weightless, floating an inch or two above the back seat. Besides astronauts and other people who've flown in NASA's "vomit comet," I'm probably one of the few people on this planet who has experienced weightlessness.) Believe me, it is a joy, and we did it lots and lots of times—whenever I could cajole Daddy into doing it. In retrospect, I realize it WAS dangerous, but I liked it so much!

Mother says in her writings that I complained because we always flew, and asked why we couldn't take the train like other people. You have to remember that this was the early '50's—the Eisenhower era—and what were eventually to become the interstate highways were just beginning to be built. Back then, trains were THE epitome of luxury, travel-wise, and there I was: stuck in a four-foot, smelly back seat for maybe an hour or two. The concept of the linear distance traveled and at what speed was totally lost on me.

There are a couple of things I didn't like about flying, other than having to get up at the crack of dawn in the cold. One was the Omni directional. The speaker was directly over the back seat, and it beep-beeped incessantly. Man, I got so sick of hearing that sound, particularly after we flew to Florida and back for my grandparent's fiftieth wedding anniversary. Days and days of beep-beep-beep. The other was the smell. Whatever glue they used to put airplanes together back then stank something awful. To this day, I can identify the odor from a mile away.

Eventually I got old enough to push the plane out of the hangar in the morning, which was a big deal for me! Hands had to be placed just so—so as not to damage the wing- or tail-flaps in any way. Then, when I was six or seven, I graduated to learning how to taxi the plane on the ground. Unfortunately, that's when my "flight school" ended because Daddy was grounded by a heart attack.

I was beginning third grade, and I remember not being able to visit him in the hospital because, back then, children carried a multitude of germs. Nevertheless, my best friend and I went on an after-school search for Daddy's favorite thing: black licorice jelly beans. We eventually found a bag (no small feat in a very small town), but we'd missed our after-school bus, so we decided to walk home to her house, which was a mere two miles from town, as opposed to the five miles to my house. Well, after the sheriff had been sent out for a search and we were finally located, walking blissfully and proudly with our treasure of black jelly beans, we got into a heap of trouble.

Shortly thereafter, we moved to Hawaii for three months, not because of my indiscretion but to allow Daddy to heal and recuperate.

After we returned to Cortez, Mother and Daddy still flew, but the combination of his health and the increasing air traffic made it less fun. However, Daddy made one final "emergency" trip just for me. After reading a book about seeing-eye dogs, I had become obsessed with owning a German Shepherd. So one Christmas he found a purebred puppy in Albuquerque and flew there on Christmas Eve to pick it up. As I learned later, the dog cried the whole time and pooped all over the back seat of the airplane during the return trip.

Ten years earlier on the same day, he'd flown a crying, pooping, infant baby girl to her new home to be with her new parents!

FAMILY PETS
AND OTHER ADVENTURES

Perhaps because aviation was still in the early stages, there was a closeness between those who were pilots and those who took care of the planes. We were like one happy family.

We even had "family" pets. We had a white kitten at the airport that we named "Grease Ball" because she would be around the hangars and would always have some grease on her fur. She would, also, try to sneak into the airplanes for a ride whenever she could do so unnoticed.

The mechanic, Mac, and his wife had a small bulldog, who, one day, was out in the sage brush and brought home a tiny cottontail rabbit, put it in her box, and took care of it as though it were a puppy. A few days later she came back with another one and was very protective of them for a week or more. Then she went out hunting again, and this time came back with a jack rabbit. This rabbit was larger than the cottontails and had huge upright ears. It looked so out of place in the box with the smaller ones that we were all amused. Apparently, the jack rabbit had a disease and, within two days, all of them died, and you could tell the dog was in mourning over their deaths. This is just a side-story to incidents but some things just stay with me and I can still see that very sad-faced bulldog.

We were given a mynah bird and put it in a cage outside the mechanic's home. We were told that if we split its tongue, it could be taught to talk. Each morning when I came down to the airport, I would call "Hi" to Mac, the mechanic, to let him know I had arrived and then stopped to talk to the mynah bird for a few minutes. I was trying to teach it to say, "Hi, Polly," but the bird would look at me and say quite loudly, "Hi Mac!" And that was the only time it ever talked. I kept trying to convince it that my name was Polly but with no success!

On a charter trip one day, Rollin had a forced landing at Many Farms. He phoned me at our airport to have me come and bring him back home. He assured me that I could land in the field next to his plane and gave me the directions. So leaving Wendy with the mechanic's wife, I took off in a small plane to make the rescue. When I reached the destination, I was flattered that he though I could land in such a small field, but since there was no other choice, I made a successful touchdown, and we flew back home.

Later we drove down to that area, stayed in a lodge there and visited the Indian ruins along the cliffs. It was, also, an opportunity to thank the people who had been helpful when we had landed there.

The Polly Usher Story

Not long after that, I had my third forced landing. Our mechanic had finished overhauling the engine on a plane and wanted me to fly it to our flight school in Blanding, Utah, which was about sixty miles away over isolated country. I was able to get the young girl who often stayed with Wendy to come in and take care of her so I could leave. However, she said that she had to be at a Rainbow Girl's meeting at two o'clock, which gave me two hours for the flight and return trip. Before I took off, I said to the mechanic, "This plane had better be in good shape as I am concerned that my baby sitter might leave the baby alone if I am not back in two hours." He assured me that it was in top shape, so I took off. I was only twenty minutes into my flight when a spark plug flew out through the engine cowling. Now what to do? Rollin had always told me that if ever I was in trouble in that area to head for the river, and he would look for me there. I was headed toward the McElmo River when I noticed a man on a tractor plowing a field just below me. He was surprised when I landed beside him. After I told him that I had to get to a telephone, I rode seventeen miles on the back of his tractor to his home, and called Rollin to get the baby and then come to pick me up. The farmer's wife was baking homemade bread when I arrived, so while I was waiting, I had some delicious bread, butter, and jam.

Indeed, I have been so fortunate in some of my adventures, and I shall never cease to admire the thoughtfulness of people everywhere.

ARRESTED!

With the completion of the Civil Pilot Training Program, we no longer needed extra flight instructors, and Frank Brgoch obtained a position as an airline pilot. The last time I saw him was when I happened to be at the airport in Salt Lake City. I heard someone say, "Hi Polly," and looked up to see this 5-foot-6-inch handsome Frank sitting at the controls of this large airplane with a big smile on his face. Later, I was told that he passed away, so perhaps his urge to sleep a lot when he was working for us was an indication of a health problem.

We also had more time for our own pleasure trips. When Wendy was four years old, we decided to take a week's vacation at a resort hotel in Guymas, Mexico. We took off in our plane, landing at Nogales, Arizona, to obtain permission for entrance into Mexico and instructions on the procedure to follow on our return trip. We were told just to stop and check in on our return as we had done on entering.

The resort was lovely and relaxing. Each day we would take a boat trip to a different restaurant along the bay for luncheon. Our hotel had music, entertainment, and dancing in the evening. The waiters and waitresses were charmed with Wendy and treated her like a princess. The carefree atmosphere made us quite reluctant to leave when the week was concluded, but we took off as scheduled for our return trip.

Upon landing at Nogales, as we had been instructed to do, we were surprised to be greeted by armed law enforcement officers. Before we could get out of the airplane, we were arrested for entering the United States illegally! Rollin, from his experience as bank examiner and banker, had a very positive demeanor when he needed it. He insisted that Wendy and I be free to go have some lunch, and they could take him into the office for cross-examination.

He was arguing with the officers for a couple of hours. They referred to an old law that pertained to "ships at sea" requiring them to contact shore before landing. Rollin countered that we had no way to contact the airport from the airplane, and no phone service existed between Guymas and Nogales at that time. Besides that, we were following the instructions we had received upon leaving the United States. He was informed that if he paid a fine, we would be released. Being a stubborn and principled person, he did not want to do that but eventually decided it was going to be the only solution. So he paid the fine as they requested.

The Polly Usher Story

It was near dusk when we were free to leave, but Rollin was determined not to spend the night there and wanted to fly to the nearest stateside airport. However, there was a little vibration in the engine as he was checking the aircraft for takeoff. Now was a time for serious thinking. The engine was not functioning properly, night was approaching, and he was not in a good mood. It did not seem to be a judicious decision to risk the lives of his wife and daughter. Consequently, we taxied back to the office and spent the night in a nearby motel and flew home safely the next day. Immediately, Rollin contacted the Airplane Owners and Pilot's Association who checked into the border old-time law being used and had it rescinded. So perhaps he saved others from having a similar distressing experience.

FATHER

My father had retired from the construction business in Denver, and they had moved to Florida. When WWII came along and my three brothers enlisted in the service for their country, my father realized that when the war was over, they might have difficulty in finding employment, so he started up a construction business in Florida—building a hospital, church, and homes until my brothers returned and took over the business.

On my parent's fiftieth anniversary, October 28, 1955, we flew to Florida to be with all of the family members for a joyous celebration. A party was held in a private dining room at a lovely hotel, and each of us made some speech or performance that reflected our happy family life.

Dad was the life of the party, and we all requested him to sing a Danish song that he had sung for us many times when we were children. He sang it in the Danish language with many gestures, and it always made us laugh. He sang it again at the anniversary with the same result. It was as if we had never heard it before, and we enjoyed every phrase, which we never would have understood if he hadn't explained it to us in English when we were little.

After dinner my brothers got into a discussion about which of them had the best looking legs. They each rolled up their pant legs and posed for a picture, like a chorus line. All the legs looked good, so we couldn't make a decision.

The party ended about midnight after a toast to our wonderful parents, and we went back to their home where we were staying and went to bed. A few hours later, we were awakened as my father had become ill. A doctor lived not too far away, and came as soon as he was called. He diagnosed a heart attack, and an ambulance was called, and Dad was transported to the hospital—the hospital he had constructed.

The whole family soon gathered at the hospital. It was a time of great concern, and we were grateful for being together at such a momentous time. Dad's condition remained stable for several hours, and we were all hopeful. When lunch time came, I volunteered to stay at the hospital with Mother while the rest of the group went out for some food.

Mother and I sat beside Father's bed, holding hands and talking quietly about what a wonderful man he was. Within a short time there was a feeling of peace in the room. Dad gave a gentle sigh and was gone. When I thought it was nearly time for the rest of the family to return from lunch, I walked out to the front of the hospital to meet them and give them the news. They went on in to give their love and support to Mother. We all spent another week there, funeral services were held, and we all felt that, indeed, God had been in direct charge of all events. No one could have planned it more efficiently. My sister Oda volunteered to stay with Mother, who lived only two more years and then went to join her beloved husband—my dad. The rest of the family returned to their own lives, thankful for having shared a beautiful anniversary for our parents and the time we all had together.

MORE FOREIGN CONNECTIONS

The first air mail flight to Cortez was on August 14, 1949, and again we gave ourselves a pat on the back for having established an airport in our area.

Because we were strategically located, we had many well known people landing at our field. Adolph Coors, the owner of Coors Brewery in Golden, Colorado, stopped one day. We loaned him our car so that he could visit Mesa Verde National Park. On his return home he sent me three different size baking dishes from their pottery plant. They have been my favorite baking dishes for more than fifty years, and my daughter has her eye on them for when I no longer need them.

Flying Joyfully

One early morning we thought we had a visitor from outer space, as we awakened to see a very strange looking plane on the Runway. Rollin immediately rushed down to the airport to investigate. It turned out to be a U-2 spy plane. This was nine months before Gary Powers was shot down over Europe and before any civilians knew such an aircraft existed. It was built by Lockheed, but to keep extreme secrecy, our government hired a pilot from the Chinese Air Force to fly it. On August 4, 1959, Major Hau was flying the U-2 when he had a flame-out over Ogden, Utah. He was flying at an altitude of 70,000 feet at 10:30 p.m. The only ground lights he could see were at the Cortez Airport, many miles away. Rollin always insisted that the runway lights be left on all night, as it might just save a life. The pilot was able to glide that far and land safely. The Air Force was advised immediately and flew in an enormous transport plane. Our airport was secured tightly from onlookers while the top secret camera was removed and the U-2 dismantled and flown out on the transport plane. We loaned the pilot our car while he was there, and he gave us his business card, written in Chinese, for us to put in a Taiwan newspaper if we ever got there. He said that he had lots of relatives and someone would see it and he would come find us. Unfortunately, we never managed to accept his invitation.

We did accept another gracious invitation, however, when friends in Cortez had residents from Bermuda visiting them. Their names were Mr. and Mrs. Trimmingham, and they owned a large department store in Bermuda. The British government, at that time, would allow citizens leaving the island to take only a limited amount of money with them, so while in Cortez, the Trimminghams found themselves short of cash. They were such a delightful couple, and we enjoyed showing them our part of the world. We flew them to

Monument Valley for a day's trip. They were impressed with the spectacular scenery and the people they met there. Before they left Colorado, they invited us to visit them in Bermuda and stay in their guest house.

Wendy was not yet of school age, and we had enough employees to take care of the airport, so we were free to takeoff in our plane and fly to Miami a short time later. There we boarded an airline for Bermuda. There were few passengers on the plane, and Rollin had told the pilot that I was a flight instructor. As soon as the plane was in the air and had reached cruising altitude and was on course, the pilot invited me into the cockpit to take over the controls. It was quite an experience, being in charge of such a large plane. I had no idea what all the instruments were for, but I managed to stay on course and fly straight and level for some time. Both the pilot and the copilot complimented me as I left the cockpit, and I thanked them profusely for such a unique experience.

We had a short stop in Havana, Cuba, where we were given rum drinks to ensure we had a happy flight. It is quite evident that flying in those days was a much more relaxed atmosphere than it is now.

Our friends in Bermuda met us at the airport and took us to their lovely guest house, which had a well-stocked bar, food in the refrigerator, and a maid who came in every morning to fix our breakfast for us.

One day Mr. Trimmingham, invited us to see his department store and have lunch with him at his club. We dressed in what we thought would be proper clothing for luncheon at the club and took a short boat trip to the store location. When Mr. Trimmingham greeted us, he looked very handsome in Bermuda shorts, shirt, and tie. He told Rollin that he could not go to the club without wearing a tie. Rollin laughed and said, "You mean you can go in short pants, but I have to wear a tie?" The answer was "yes," and Mr. Trimmingham went into the Men's Department and picked out a beautiful tie and gave it to Rollin. It turned out to be Rollin's favorite, and he did wear it quite often whenever the situation demanded it.

I was most impressed with the Trimmingham Department Store, and purchased some clothes there that I was quite proud of. Recently, a close friend visited Bermuda and sent me some golf balls with the Trimmingham logo on them. Knowing where they came from, I expect them to go a long way when I "swing"! She also told me that the store had expanded, and the business is now operated by the grandsons.

KAUAI

NIIHAU

OAHU

MOLOKAI

Honolulu

LANAI

MAUI

KAHOOLAWE

HAWAII

HAWAII

ALOHA SPIRIT

Rollin's second passion after flying was fly fishing, so on some weekends we would take Wendy and Carol Lynne and go to a lodge on the Dolores River where he could fish to his heart's content, the girls could play along the river, and the food was absolutely delicious.

One day, however, while he was fishing, he suffered a heart attack and was taken to the hospital in Cortez for recuperation. While he was there, he did some re-thinking about his life. When I would visit him, he would relate that there were still places that he wanted to visit—mainly Hawaii but also places in the South Pacific such as Tahiti, Bora-Bora, and Fiji. When his body stabilized and he was released from the hospital, we made plans to begin fulfilling his desires and thought Hawaii would be a good place to start.

Wendy was in the third grade. Our minister referred us to a school the Episcopal Church has in Honolulu—St. Andrew's Priory—and we were able to enroll her there. Through a friend, we located a two-story house on the beach at Diamond Head for five hundred dollars a month, which included a Hawaiian maid, who would do the cooking and house cleaning, and a gardener to take care of the one-acre yard. We purchased our airline tickets—Wendy and I put on our best dresses, hat, and gloves, Rollin wore a suit (no tie), and we were off to "paradise".

Our first stop was San Francisco, where we spent the night at the beautiful Mark Hopkins Hotel, had dinner at the Top of the Mark, where we watched the boats coming into the harbor, and had a wonderful meal. On the next day we started our twelve-hour trip across the Pacific. It was before jet airplanes, so the flight was long. But because there were few passengers, we could stretch out, and relax in the aircraft. There were even a few berths where one could lie down and take a nap. On our return trip, we had learned from the Hawaiians how to be comfortable, so as soon as we got on the plane, we changed from our dress clothes to a muu-muu and enjoyed the flight.

Upon arriving at the Honolulu Airport, since there was no building there, we stood on the tarmac while our luggage was being unloaded. An employee put a plumeria lei around our necks, and we were off to our lovely home at Diamond Head. Then it started to rain and didn't quit for two weeks! There was no heat in this large, lovely home, so the only way we could get warm was to soak in a hot tub of water. Our sympathies were with some of the people we had talked to on the plane—two of whom had planned a ten-day honeymoon. But since we were to be there six months, we were not concerned about ourselves. Then the rain stopped and the beautiful tropical sunshine started. We didn't have rain again during the rest of our sojourn.

A friend at home had given us the name and address of a Hawaiian couple, and as soon as we contacted them we became part of the family. They were a handsome couple—Lillian and Harold Hewit, and had a beautiful eighteen-year-old daughter who danced with Hilo Hatties Hula Dancers. When she was a baby her daddy called her "Sweetie Pie," which soon changed to "Pie" as she got older. It was not long until she had Wendy in a grass skirt and had taught her to dance the hula.

Every Sunday we would all attend the Episcopal Church, then change into casual clothes, and spend the rest of the day making trips around the island. We soon called it, "eating our way around the island." First we would stop at a road-stand to purchase a large bag of boiled peanuts, then at a farm to get some island apples. At the top of a view point, we would watch the surfers coming in on high waves while we munched away on apples and peanuts.

We would visit the high waterfalls where swimmers dived from the top of the falls to the pool below. Here we would eat a lunch that our friends had prepared, then drive leisurely to the other side of the island, stopping at interesting spots along the way. Then we would come to the pineapple fields, where we would watch the harvesting, and eat freshly picked pineapple. When the day ended, we would make one last stop for ice cream cones. This was a Sunday ritual which we enjoyed each week for six months!.

We had told our family and friends that we would be in Hawaii for the winter and had invited them to visit, little realizing just how many would accept the invitation! We had friends arriving that we hadn't seen in twenty years, and of course, most of the family visited with us.

On long weekends and whenever Wendy had a short vacation from school, we would travel to other islands and visited all but Lanai, as it did not have an airport, and Molakai which was a leper colony at that time.

When the six months were over and school was out for the summer, we prepared to leave, with reluctance, but definitely knew this would not be our last trip to paradise. Pie, our eighteen-year-old Hawaiian friend, seemed like a daughter to us by now, and since she had never been to the continental United States, we invited her to come with us to see our part of the country. She eagerly accepted, and we loved the time she spent with us. She is still very dear to my heart, and we get together whenever I go back to the islands. Every Christmas she sends me a calendar with beautiful pictures of Hawaii. It hangs above my desk where I can re-live many wonderful memories of Hawaii every day.

When we were ready to take off from Honolulu Airport, we were given lei after lei from our friends there until they came up from our shoulders to our nose. After we got on the plane, the airline hostess put them in a cool place for us, and as we were approaching for a landing in Cortez, we put them back around our shoulders again.

Never had we experienced the wonderful hospitality and friendliness that we found on The Island. There were few visitors from the mainland, and we were greeted with open arms by the people who lived there. They explained to us that this was the "aloha spirit," and we loved it.

We were astounded at the large group of people who had assembled on the ground at the Cortez Airport waiting to welcome us home. Being the first in the area to go to Hawaii, we were famous! We had enough leis to put one around the neck of each person who was there to greet us, and it was a very, very happy homecoming.

We were delighted a short time later when Pie's parents, Harold and Lillian, came for a visit. We flew them down to Monument Valley one day, and Harry Goulding took all of us on a tour of the valley, ending up at the medicine man's hogan for a sand painting. The Navajo Indians felt there was some connection between their ancestors and the Hawaiians and were most interested in our guests.

The medicine man put Lillian and Harold together at one end of the hogan where they sat on the ground, cross-legged, in an up-right posture—a very handsome sight. Then he positioned himself opposite them on the other end of the hogan, with room in the middle of the sand painting. The rest of us arranged ourselves on the floor, making a circle around the dwelling. He then started on another spectacular arrangement of the colored sand into an original painting. Each one is so different from the other that one wishes there were some way to preserve it rather than have it destroyed, but that would not be a part of the ancient ceremony.

This day when the painting was completed, the medicine man did his chanting and then indicated that he would like to have Lillian and Harold sing a Hawaiian song. They looked at me rather perplexed, and I suggested the Hawaiian wedding song, which I had heard them perform so beautifully many times. There are no words to express the feelings in that mud hogan with three cultures brought together in that small space and the blending together of the beautiful voices of such an attractive couple singing the Hawaiian wedding song. There was complete silence for many moments after the last tone sounded, then the sand painting was reverently erased by the hands of the medicine man, and we quietly left the hogan.

Our visit to Hawaii was so soul-satisfying that we decided it was time to sell our flying service and move on to fulfill more dreams. We sold the flight school and planes to an interested buyer, who had a young son who would later become a talented pilot himself. We kept only the Beechcraft Bonanza for our own transportation and pleasure.

The following winter we returned to Hawaii again where Wendy once again attended the Episcopal school. The rent on the house at Diamond Head had increased substantially. Consequently, we decided to stay at the lovely Waikikian Hotel instead. It was a delightful place, with a swimming pool and outdoor patio for dining. Wendy took swimming lessons from a young Hawaiian boy and became a beautiful swimmer. We enjoyed watching her graceful strokes across the pool, which she seem to accomplish so easily.

Instead of taking a tour around the island each Sunday, we went to the fabulous brunch at the elegant Royal Hawaiian Hotel. When I visited there again with Pie, a few years ago, it had not changed in the intervening fifty years, and it was easy for me to go back in time.

While we were in Honolulu, we received word that Rollin's mother had passed away, and we made a return trip to Colorado. His father had died two years previously, and she had not been happy without her beloved husband.

When we were there, I saw a man, who from Rollin's description over the years, I knew must be the "town character"—Taos McCandles—and it was. Rollin introduced me to him, and he told me that he was on his way to purchase a light bulb, as he had been reading in bed the night before, and hadn't felt like getting out of bed to turn off the light, so he had taken the BB gun beside his bed and shot out the light. Now he needed to replace it—and I don't think he had changed much at all over the years!

At age fifty-five, Rollin decided that he wanted to retire but didn't feel that he could do so and still remain in Cortez. I didn't want to leave as I felt we were so much a part of the community, and I was a Colorado girl. However, he always had a delightful way of changing my decisions. He took Wendy and me to the lovely town of La Jolla, California. There we found an attractive home for sale with a beautiful rose garden in bloom. Bishop School was nearby where Wendy could enroll for her high school years, so I agreed that I could be happy there also.

We sold our home in Cortez along with our Beechcraft Bonanza. Because of his heart problems, Rollin could no longer pass the health examination for his pilot's license, and I felt that I did not want to fly in the San Diego area with multiple airplanes flying around, creating heavy air traffic.

Rollin also gave the airport land back to the county. The town of Cortez was greatly influenced by this wonderful man—my husband! Under his supervision the Citizens State Bank was a great contributor to the growth of the community, and because of our devotion to flying, the area has a functional county airport. Before leaving, a party of farewell was given in his honor. He was presented with a plaque commending him for his outstanding service and personal contribution to the community. Today, that plaque still hangs in a prominent place in my home.

SOUTH PACIFIC
DREAMS COME TRUE

La Jolla turned out to be a most friendly place and we became acquainted with many interesting people. We attended parties where we met the author of the Dr. Seuss books (Theodor Geisel), a most interesting man, and others, who made conversation around the dinner table very uplifting.

Wendy was soon a member of the water ballet group at school, which put on a lovely graceful demonstration. I was so proud of our daughter and marveled at how quickly she was growing up to be a fine young lady.

Rollin and I took up golf in the same dedicated way we had learned to fly. One of the early professional golfers, Paul Runyan taught the women's beginning group at La Jolla Country Club, named the "Happy Hackers."

He insisted that we be most diligent in learning the short-game skills. When learning sand-trap shots, he would say, "Don't just think of getting the ball out of the sand trap; think of getting it out of the sand into the cup." He repeated this many times to reinforce it in our minds. I remember one time on my birthday when I finally did accomplish that.

Paul Runyan died at the age of ninety-three. He played eighteen holes of golf every day until the last few months of his life. I was playing golf in Palm Desert the day I heard of his death. He was in my thoughts as I played the course. My ball went into a deep bunker, and I had doubts that I would be able to get it out but decided to give it a try. I don't even remember hitting the ball, but it went neatly out of the sand, took one bounce, and went into the cup. I looked up to the sky and said, "Thank you Paul Runyon." It definitely was not negotiated by any skill of mine.

When Wendy's summer vacation came, we were off on our trip to Tahiti and were on the FIRST airline flight to that island. We were three of ten people on board Air France for the initial flight. After we reached flying altitude, we were served champagne, and the host and hostesses pushed a cart down the aisle cutting slices of a large roast of beef to our individual taste, along with vegetables and rolls. Then later, a dessert cart came along with a variety to choose from. Believe me, the finest hotel could not have served a more perfect meal.

We landed in Tahiti after dark, and since the airport did not have ground lights, there were several cars parked along the side shining their car lights onto the runway so the pilot could safely land the plane.

The Polly Usher Story

We were taken to the lovely Tahitian Hotel where the sheets were turned back on our beds and we were each given colorfully designed kimonos. What a truly happy place this was. There was a lovely outdoor patio where each meal was served and where we could sit and enjoy the splendor of the Island.

The movie "Mutiny on the Bounty" was being filmed there at the time, and each morning while we were eating breakfast, we would see the ship and the actors going out to the location at sea and returning later that evening. The members of the cast were staying at the same hotel where we were, and they were always very relaxed and friendly. I think it would be impossible to be otherwise in that lovely atmosphere in Tahiti.

Each evening the natives would run out, scantily clad, with flaming torches to light the stationary torches placed around the hotel. It was a beautiful sight and one we looked forward to. Natives performed their spectacular dances to the beat of the drums both at lunch and dinner.

From Tahiti we took a flying boat to Bora Bora. The pilot was a large muscular man, and we weren't sure if leaving the fly open on his trousers was by mistake or on purpose! We spent two days on the beach at Bora Bora, snorkling, relaxing, and watching the full moon come up at night.

Then on to Fiji. Each island was different from the other. We had to keep pinching ourselves to believe that we were really there in the midst of all this beautiful and interesting scenery.

In Fiji, we were fascinated with the large men with tall hats who directed the endless traffic. They were so forceful in their directions that I can't imagine anyone not stopping when they held their hand up to indicate "STOP."

We were fortunate to be invited to a native ceremony which reminded us of those we had attended in the hogans on the Navajo reservation. It was held in a small hut, and we sat in a circle on the ground while the ceremony was performed. The difference was that the leader mixed up a drink called "kava," in which he added various herbs and then passed around the circle for each one present to take a sip. After more chanting, the kava was passed around the circle again. It had a very strange taste, and we didn't realize that it was also somewhat mind affecting. When Wendy and I got up to leave the hut, we had to hold on to each other for a few minutes to steady ourselves. This was, however, not a down moment on this part of our trip as we were most thankful to have had this unusual experience.

THE FAMILY GROWS

One day in La Jolla, Wendy came home from school with a big smile on her face and a Siamese kitten in her arms, promising she would take care of it if she could keep it. We named the kitten Susu, and as it turned out, she more or less took care of herself and soon let us know who was in charge of the household.

We fixed a little bed for her and a sandbox in our utility room, where she spent the nights. One night I forgot to bring her sandbox in from out of doors, and the next morning I was surprised to discover she had used the toilet, which was located in the utility room. From that time on, she had no use for her sandbox. If we were to be away from home for a few days, we would ask a friend to come into the house to leave food and flush the toilet!

Wendy graduated from Bishop School and, after a few years in college, married and moved to the Bay Area. The damp weather near the coast was beginning to have a negative effect on Rollin's health, so we made plans to move to the desert. We had visited Gretchen and Jimmy Swinnerton in Palm Desert, California, several times and knew that we liked the area. We purchased a home, which had a swimming pool, and it was located near a golf course. Now, I could swim in the pool and look up at the ten-thousand-foot mountains. It was also a very delightful place for our family to visit.

My first lovely granddaughter, Erika, was born in 1970; the second, Michelle, was born five years later. I spent the first ten days of their lives with them—holding, bathing, and hugging them and enjoying another dream of mine fulfilled. When they came to the desert to visit, I would take them in to the pool. They took to the water like fish and could swim even as infants. It was remarkable. For years one of my greatest enjoyments was reading children's books to them, where they would sit and listen totally absorbed in the story. When they learned to read for themselves, I always had many books available for them to read.

When my granddaughter Erika married her wonderful husband, Tristan, they moved to the desert to be near me, and Michelle comes to visit at every opportunity. We have a close relationship, and in many ways, I could not get along without them.

Rollin and I enjoyed our house with the pool during the winter months and went back to Cortez for the summer. We would visit with our dear old-time friends in an area we both still loved and was very dear to both of us.

After ten years, we started to look around for a house that would require less care and found a perfect place in Palm Desert where we felt we could spend the rest of our years. It is located on a beautiful golf course in a gated community, which offered good security and had available, tennis courts, swimming pools, and other facilities for sports and, of course, a free eighteen-hole executive golf course.

We continued to spend our summers in Cortez, Colorado, and in 1979 on our return trip, we detoured to spend a night in the town of Laughlin, Nevada, where there was a small hotel on the river that had a room for gambling. Rollin played roulette that evening and won six hundred dollars. He was so excited that, when he got back home, he called a friend in Cortez to tell him of his good luck. His friend said, "Well, then, you can afford to buy a hundred dollar raffle ticket on a Lincoln Continental automobile. The proceeds are to be used to build a golf course in Cortez." Rollin readily agreed, happy, again, to be part of a community project.

A few weeks later he received a phone call at eleven o'clock at night to tell him that he had won a white Lincoln Continental car. We lost little time in going back to possess it. Then we happily drove through the northern part of California to show it to our daughter, Wendy, and our granddaughters before returning home.

We were humbled to have been so fortunate. I rather felt as though it was really a bonus, which Rollin deserved for his service to that community and that it really added a few more years to his life. Indeed, he was beginning to give in to poor health, but the new beautiful car gave him an incentive to travel some more, and we continued to spend our summers in Colorado. We took such excellent care of the Lincoln, having it washed, waxed, and properly serviced, that when I donated it to charity twenty-three years later, it still looked like new!

EISENHOWER MEDICAL CENTER

Service Award

Presented to *Pauline Usher*

In Recognition of (5) years of service

MAY 12, 1977

Dolores Hope

Chairman of the Board

Palm Desert residents honored

Palm Desert residents who were honored at a recent dinner at the Palm Springs Pavilion for their five years of service to Eisenhower Medical Center are, front row (left), Donna MacNeil, LaFrieta Metzler,   Fernetta Bowles, Gladys Bosler, Alison Hansen Rose Phillips. Back row, Joe Russell, Kathy Charles Gill, Pauline Usher, Maggie Leon and Higdon.

WINDING DOWN

Life in Palm Desert Greens was easy and pleasant, but I began to feel that I needed a little more challenge than just playing bridge and trying to improve my golf game. A hospital had just been built in the area—Eisenhower Medical Center. I applied for a job in the Nursing Administration Office and was accepted. I enjoyed the years I worked there under such caring, qualified people, who are still my friends. Donna, who did the scheduling of hospital employees, is one of my closest friends even now, and we do many interesting things together, even spending time in her condo in Hawaii.

Rollin had always liked to cook and took over the grocery shopping and preparing meals, so I completely enjoyed the ten years of hospital work. Then, as it became more difficult for Rollin to get out of bed each day, I realized that I needed to stay home and take care of him, so I terminated my job at the hospital and happily assumed the responsibility of caring for Rollin.

He was such a wonderful patient and so appreciative of each thing I did for him that it was never a chore. If he awakened in the night and wanted food, I would get up and prepare whatever would taste good to him. If he just wanted to talk, I would listen. It was a winding down of the forty-six years we had been together. Often he would say, "You are so good to me. Someday I am going to give you something really nice." I would respond, "What could you give me that I don't already have?"

One morning I had a call from Mike Goulding of Monument Valley. Her husband Harry had died a few years previously. Mike was in California with her brother and wanted to come by for a short visit. I went to Rollin's bedside and asked him if he felt up to having company. He said, "I would love to see Mike again. Tell them to come," which I did. Then I proceeded to bake some cookies. They arrived a few hours later. Rollin got out of bed, and the four of us sat around the table eating cookies, chatting, and laughing. I was amazed at how vibrant Rollin was—talking about things we had enjoyed together at Monument Valley, and laughing again about knocking the chimney off their home with the wing of his plane. We were all sorry when it was time for them to leave.

After their departure, Rollin went immediately to bed, and I walked out onto the patio to think over the pleasant afternoon. How could Rollin be so ill, then get out of bed and be the life of the party? Perhaps I was being too attentive and should encourage him to get out of bed more often. I walked back into the house to find him standing by the bed. He immediately crumbled over and was dead—and I had left him only for a few minutes!

Wendy came to be with me, and our grandchildren and his family were there to take care of the food, refreshments, and memorial service. All went just as he would have wanted it.

When the day was over, I felt a sudden desire to go to bed early and said good night to Wendy. After I had slept a couple of hours, I awakened with a wonderful feeling of peace. I sat up on the side of the bed, and Rollin's voice said to me, "This peace is what I want you to have for the devotion you showed to me."

I remarked, "But what about my leaving you for the last few minutes of your life?"

"Well," he replied, "that shows you are not perfect, but now I have to leave."

I agreed, and his spirit left, but the wonderful peace has remained with me.

LIFE ON MY OWN

I have always had a close relationship with my step-granddaughter, Rhonda. She and her wonderful husband, Dick, had a winter home in Hawaii, on the Island of Maui, where they invited me to visit each year. Soon, there I was, once again spending happy days golfing, being on the beach, and watching the sun set over the ocean each evening. I would watch to see if there was a final green flash as the sun disappeared out of sight. Being in a place I have loved since Rollin and I visited there many years ago was a very, very heart-warming experience.

Even though I enjoy the company of men friends and considered re-marriage a few times, I just couldn't envision a union that would have been as precious as the one I had with Rollin. Perhaps, also, I was concerned that having someone else in my life might cause me to lose the deep closeness I have with my daughter and granddaughters, as they definitely are my treasures. So I started going back to Cortez, Colorado for the summer months to try to establish a pattern for living my life alone.

On my drive to Colorado, I decided to stop to visit Mike Goulding at Monument Valley. As soon as I came into Indian country, I felt such a wonderful peace and strength, and wonderful memories of the times we had spent there flooded my mind. I loved being with Mike again, and the few hours we were together were spent reminiscing. We went through the old trading post and museum saying, "Remember this; remember that?" and talking about how much laughter had been part of our times together.

In Cortez, I rented a small house near the edge of McElmo Canyon. I would go to the edge of the canyon every morning just to sit peacefully or to write down my feelings. The scenery was spectacular. The cactus was in full bloom, their colors so vibrant, tucked against a rock or dead cedar tree stump.

Each day as I started down the trail to the canyon, I would be joined by a small fox. He would follow me to the edge of the canyon and sit on a rock nearby, facing me. He would stay there as long as I did, either silent or talking to me in "fox language." I could take his picture or talk to him, and he seemed to enjoy the connection.

One morning I was standing on the edge of the canyon, just admiring the scenery. I felt something gently brush against my ankle. I looked down to see a baby skunk rubbing against me as though offering its sympathy. I carefully walked away so as not to disturb it, just in case it decided to share its "scent" also.

I never tired of sitting on the rim of the canyon alone. I would be there for hours, morning and evening and even into the night hours, watching a full moon. I have fed chipmunks and seen deer. I discovered that there is a sanctuary within me where I can retreat to at anytime and be my true self.

A group of friends had been going to Lake Powell each summer to spend a week on the lake in a houseboat. They invited me to go with them, and it was a fun experience to travel the lake with the closeness of a congenial group—ten of us. We slept in berths or sleeping bags, shared one tiny bathroom, and ate good food. On looking up at the canyon walls, I was also aware of the beautiful canyons below the lake surface that Rollin and I had seen on our first trip so long ago up the Glen Canyon to Rainbow Bridge.

And then I was back to FLYING AGAIN! Several of my friends still owned their own planes and trusted me at the controls. It was an uplift for my spirits to be flying in that atmosphere again, and I never turned down an invitation. I would help wash the airplanes or whatever chores needed to be done to show my appreciation.

One day, I was entertaining four of my close lady friends for lunch when the telephone rang, and an airplane owner and friend said he had to make a trip to Durango and wondered if I would like to accompany him. I answered, "I shall be right there." So I took off for the airport leaving the ladies to finish their lunch and clean up the dishes! The important thing to me was that I got to fly a plane to Durango and back.

The young son of the owner to whom we had sold our flying service let me fly his Piper Cruiser—a three-place plane—that I had used for flight training many years previously. And then I had the exhilarating experience of flying a glider that was stationed at the airport.

149

Flying Joyfully

A tow plane took us off the ground and released the glider at about two hundred feet altitude, and the owner turned the controls over to me. I had flown light-airplanes off that airport for so many years that I knew where the updrafts and downdrafts were along the mesa. Here at the controls of the glider, I felt as though I was doing student training once again, teaching my student how to use the updrafts to gain altitude.

Our glider flight was to have been for twenty minutes, but I kept the plane climbing until we reached an altitude over 13,000 feet. I asked the owner if I should head back to the airport for landing, and he said, "No, I'm enjoying the flight as much as you are." Then he added, "You have a nice touch." We cruised around for over three hours and never have I had such a joyous flight. It was the last entry in my log book.

Through Ronda and Dick, I met a bachelor friend, Jack Kenifick, who had a two-story home on a beautiful lake in Connecticut. He enjoyed playing golf as I do, and we developed an easy friendship. When he invited me to spend a couple of the summer months at his place, I accepted readily, as I loved New England from the first time I had visited there at the age of eighteen. I was happy to have the opportunity to spend time in that beautiful scenery again.

Arriving there from the hot desert temperatures, I was overwhelmed with the beauty of the many trees and how green everything was. I soon established a pattern of taking daily walks into the forest and found an isolated spot where I could sit for hours as I had done at the canyon in Colorado. I felt that same wonderful peace that comes from being a part of nature. I gazed up at the top of all the tall trees and felt a connection with all my family—especially Rollin—and friends who had passed on to a better life, and somehow I recognized a sort of encouragement they were giving me.

I also became absorbed in watching the birds, butterflies, and insects. One day a beautiful blue dragonfly landed on the palm of my hand. It sat there for several minutes as I admired the colors and shape of its body; then it flew away. The next day when I was sitting there it came back again and followed the same routine. This happened for several days in a row. Then one day there was a light rain falling, but that did not deter me from my usual walk, and I always felt a certain energy boost from the rain. As I sat in the forest, I wondered if the dragonfly would come, and it did, shaking the rain drops from its body just as though it were saying, "I made it." That was the last time I saw my lovely beautiful blue dragonfly, but I have heard that they are short lived.

Besides walking in the forest, I loved swimming in the lake, floating on my back and looking up at the clouds that are so unique to New England. I had seen them in Maxfield Parrish's painting in books that I read as a child. There was a private airport nearby, so I enjoyed watching and hearing the small aircraft that flew overhead—wishing all the while that I could be at the controls!

For a while I also continued to spend part of my summer in Cortez, and the rest of the summer in Connecticut. Then my friends in Colorado sold their planes and were not too interested in golf, so I went to Connecticut for the three summer months, becoming part of the lovely, caring family there and making lasting friendships that I treasure dearly.

Flying Joyfully

Coming back home to Palm Desert, California, for the winter months made a wonderful pattern for living. I enjoy the mild winter weather in the desert, and since my home is on the golf course, the view is delightful and I can play golf!

One day a friend who knew I had done some flying in my earlier days asked me if I would consider giving a talk about my flying experiences to her sorority group. I was petrified at the thought, but since I can never turn down a challenge, I agreed to do it. I started going through my flight log books and scrapbooks and soon had enough material for a twenty-minute talk.

When I got up in front of the group on the appointed day, I started out by telling them that I would feel more comfortable landing a light aircraft on a busy highway than I felt trying to give a speech. However, as I progressed and saw the interest on each of the faces, it became easier, and when I finished, the applause seemed genuine.

The next day I received a phone call from one of the ladies who had been present the day before, requesting that I speak to another group. It went on from there. Women told their husbands about my experiences, and I was invited to be a guest speaker at the Optimist Club, Rotary Club, and others. Each time I was a little apprehensive, and each time the interest on the faces in the audience gave me reassurance.

Later, I was invited back to Cortez where several men, whom I had taught to fly and to whom I had given their licenses, brought along their log books for me to sign them once again.

One of the highlights was when I went back to Denver to talk to a luncheon reunion of my high school class. It took me back to the 1930's when, with the friends present, we had enjoyed such happy, carefree days. This was a renewal of these friendships, which still continues through letters and telephone calls.

The Polly Usher Story

While in Denver, I stayed with my dearest friend of seventy-five years—Mildred. We were inseparable through junior high and high school, and still retain that close friendship although separated by many miles. I also spent time with my many nieces and nephews and their families. My niece, Lynne, took me to see my home again where I was born and to see all the homes my father had built, where we lived, even to the mountain cabin in Indian Hills where we spent the summer months growing up. It was a week of happy memories and joy.

Even in Connecticut there was an interest in hearing about flying in the early days. I was asked to talk to the Rotary Club and a Ladies Book Club. I have met so many wonderful interesting people through these contacts.

Flying will always be a passion in my life. When I heard of the activities of the Smithsonian Air and Space Museum in Washington, D. C., I was interested and supportive. Through contact with the Director of the Museum Society, Joseph Suarez, I learned that because of my early flying experiences and contribution to the growth of aviation in this country, my name would be on the Wall of Honor at the Air and Space Museum, which opened December 17, 2003. I had thought my glider flight was probably the end of my connection with aviation, but now there was the Air and Space Museum that also had asked to sell my picture to airplane businesses and airline magazines, another highlight in this wonderful life I am living. Surely the joy has been in the journey, and I continue to "Fly Joyfully."

In April of 2004, I flew to Washington, D. C. where I was met by my daughter, Wendy, and my nephew, Bill, who had made arrangements and reservations for our stay in Washington, and his wife, Ann, who live in Florida. My brother, Tom's daughter,

Janice, and handsome son, Todd, also from Florida, and my niece, Lynne and her husband from Denver joined us.

When we walked into the museum on the day our tour was scheduled, I was surprised to see a picture of me and my Stinson airplane displayed on the front desk. We were greeted by a gentleman, Mr. Kronin, who spent hours taking us through the construction where they have planes from the Wright Brothers to the present time. He pointed to my name on the Wall of Honor with the many others who have contributed to the growth of aviation. Aviation in this country has a truly rich history, and I am so thankful for having been a small part of it. My trip to the museum with some of my family was an experience that I shall treasure forever.

There was still MORE joy in my life. I would like to set down here again what I wrote in my log book on my twenty-ninth birthday:

This ends another log book, and one of the happiest years of my life. I know that I shall someday look back with pleasure on the good times and satisfaction which I have had instructing students. My students number twenty and we have eight planes. It will be interesting to note the growth of aviation in the next twenty-five years.

Sixty years later to the date (September 14, 2004), I was visiting my nephew and niece (Phil and Sally) in their lovely home in Park City, Utah. As a birthday gift they arranged for me to fly an open-cockpit bi-plane. Being at the controls, flying over the beautiful mountains again brought back many happy memories and tears to my eyes. My heart has yet to come back down to earth! *FLYING JOYFULLY*—you bet!

EPILOGUE

There we were watching the golfers aiming for that tiny little hole. We took in the magnificent view over the distant mountains, and then it happened! "Look, there goes one," I said to Polly. We both gave that longing smile as we looked up to see this small aircraft flying in the distance. "Do you suppose it's an instructor training a would-be pilot?" I said to Polly.

"Who knows?" she replied.

We gazed upwards once more; then instinctively, we both looked down at the manuscript on the table in front of us. "Well Polly," I said, "you have memories that belong only to you, and now you can share them with your readers," She gave me that gentle smile with sparkling blue eyes and a sort of devilish look and said, "You know, Marie, you're right. My life has been full, and here I am still able to watch a small plane just as I did back in 1937 when I first decided I was going to be a pilot. I was going to fly in that wonderful wild blue yonder...and I have!"

It is April 2005, and Polly enjoys her retirement, her daughter, and granddaughters and the many friends that surround her. She still gives talks about her flying experiences and delights everyone who listens. I feel fortunate to have her touch my life and share with me the joy of flying. The manuscript is on its way to the printer and soon Polly will be signing the first edition. And what a pleasure it has been for me!

Marie Robertson
Palm Springs, California